D0497532

# THE

# ASCENDED

# LIFE

**When the Position Becomes a Relationship**

*Bernita J. Conway*

Copyright 1999—Bernita J. Conway

All rights reserved. This book is protected under the copyright laws of the United States of America. This book may not be copied or reprinted for commercial gain or profit. The use of short quotations or occasional page copying for personal or group study is permitted and encouraged. Permission will be granted upon request. Unless otherwise identified, Scripture quotations are from the King James Version of the Bible. Scripture passages marked AMP are from the Amplified Bible. Selected quotes are also taken from George M. Lamsa's *Holy Bible From the Ancient Eastern Text* (New York: A.J. Holman Company, 1933, 1957, 1968). Emphasis within Scripture is the author's own.

Take note that the name satan and related names are not capitalized. We choose not to acknowledge him, even to the point of violating grammatical rules.

## Treasure House

An Imprint of
### Destiny Image® Publishers, Inc.
### P.O. Box 310
### Shippensburg, PA 17257-0310

"For where your treasure is,
there will your heart be also." Matthew 6:21

ISBN 1-56043-337-X

For Worldwide Distribution
Printed in the U.S.A.

First Printing: 1999        Second Printing: 1999

This book and all other Destiny Image, Revival Press, and Treasure House books are available
at Christian bookstores and distributors worldwide.

For a U.S. bookstore nearest you, call **1-800-722-6774**.
For more information on foreign distributors,
call **717-532-3040**.
Or reach us on the Internet: **http://www.reapernet.com**

# *Contents*

# *Endorsements*

"*The Ascended Life* leads you step by step from the foundational truths of 'Christ in us' to the glorious realities that 'we are now seated with Christ in the heavenly places.' Excellently prepared, this book grounds you in Jesus so He can launch you into exploits through His great name."

—Jim W. Goll
Author, *The Lost Art of Intercession*
Ministry to the Nations

"Dr. Conway is giving new prophetic understanding to abiding 'in Him' in her book *The Ascended Life*. Her revelations of this key phrase, 'in Him,' unlocks many doors, such as: anointing to work miracles, intimacy to know Jesus face to face, revelation to learn the mysteries of His Kingdom, power to experience divine encounters, understanding to walk in victory, ability to develop your full potential in God, personal security, and confidence to pray. In order to activate these promises, you must understand the foundational truths clearly put forth in this book!"

—Jill Austin
President, Master Potter Ministries
International and national conference speaker

# *Foreword*

Bernita Conway has been a friend for more than ten years. The longer that I have known her, the more I have come to admire her and respect her ministry. She has a strong sense of mission, and she has devoted herself to fulfilling it. She is not afraid to do it in unconventional ways, and because of this has become a part of a new breed of missionary. This new breed is now starting to give a new definition to "modern missions."

William Carey is often referred to as "the father of modern missions." He was a pioneer and spiritual father, and he helped to release a new sense of mission to the Church still emerging from the Dark Ages. Carey claimed that his inspiration came from Count Zinzendorf and the Moravians, but there were also other great spiritual pioneers, such as George White-field, John Wesley, and the courageous medical missionaries, who together gave definition to the Protestant, Evangelical, and Catholic missions that have swept the world over the past few centuries. In our times we are seeing a redefinition of missions that has the potential to usher in the greatest harvest that the world has ever seen. There are great leaders of this new wave of missions such as Loren Cunningham, Franklin Graham, Bruce Wilkinson, Bob Weiner, and many others who are well known for their missionary exploits. Then there are those like Bernita Conway, who gather small be effective teams and, with little fanfare, are accomplishing great things for the advancement of the Kingdom.

There are many who may not be well known on earth, but well known in Heaven, who are contributing to a sweeping redefinition of the expression of Christianity in our times. There are great spiritual mega-trends that are now redefining both missions and missionaries. These trends are helping to ignite great advances for the gospel.

The redefinition of missions is badly needed. The model that many are still using is archaic, based on conditions that no longer exist. Until recently, it could take a missionaries many months just to reach their mission field. This would necessarily require missionaries to stay on the field for years, maybe even for the rest of their life. With modern transportation enabling missionaries to now reach almost any place on earth within a day, it has opened up great new possibilities for effective missions, which many like Bernita Conway have understood. They have seized upon these new opportunities to accomplish great things for the Kingdom. The new breed of missionaries are becoming like Stealth bombers, learning to use speed and the ability to avoid enemy radar to drop their "smart" gospel bombs precisely on target, and then to be gone before the opposition even knows what hit them.

I have watched as Bernita would get a certain country or city in her sights. She would then assemble a small but effective team. I never once heard Bernita complain about a lack of support or resources, or about prejudice against her gender. She and her team would simply put together all that they could and trust in the Lord to make up their lack. He would. In fact, I think the Lord sees a greater opportunity to glorify His name with groups like this than through those who go with great resources. How much glory would the Lord have gotten if there was someone present with a few truckloads of food when He needed to feed the 5,000? When great resources are provided for our mission, we should be thankful, but when they are not, we should have no less doubt in the mission. Rather, we should start expecting miracles. I think that Bernita has learned this lesson, has learned the great secret of contentment, and because of this, sees many miracles.

Bernita has been a part of our fellowship for years, but she has her own spiritual well and her own sense of purpose. If she even asks us to assist with her missions, it is with no pressure or sense of urgency. When I see such pressure or urgency, it alerts me to the probability that the person is moving in his own strength. Bernita obviously has learned to lean on the Lord, not men. She is also an equipper who has led many others into a deeper, more effective walk with God.

As I read this book, I see how she has come to this place of true spiritual power—the place where there is no limit to the possibilities. Like Enoch, I know that Bernita has it in her heart to walk with God. She is an inspiration to me and many others in our fellowship, and I think that what she reveals in this book will be an inspiration to all who read it. I think that it is fitting

that I am writing this on Mother's Day, for one who is
a true "mother in Israel."

–Rick Joyner
May 9, 1999

# *Introduction*

This message developed as the result of my hunger and search to know God and to learn all that I could about Jesus, the Holy Spirit, the Father, and life. I desired to know why His relationship with me was so unique and so special.

Even as a young child, I began to talk to the Lord regarding my questions. When I was seven or eight years old, I began to compute how many years it would be until the year 2000. All of a sudden, fear gripped my heart. I was sure that I could not live that long—it was too far away. I thought that I would die before 2000. I sought the Lord desperately. It was then that He spoke to my heart and told me to be at peace, for I would live to see the year 2000. I knew then that my life would go beyond nine years old!

As I continued to inquire of the Lord, I asked Him to teach me about Heaven, for I had no understanding of that realm. One day, as I was sitting on my porch, studying the clouds as I had done when I was a child, I observed how the clouds formed and moved across the sky. The Lord then spoke to my heart and said, "When you get to Heaven, you will be *in Me*." This statement confused me. I wondered, *What does it mean that I am going to be "in God"?*

I continued to seek the Lord and asked Him to teach me more. In the months and years that went by,

He taught me how to be "in Him." I learned that through the "born-again" experience, we take our lives and translate them into His and He translates His life into ours. When we take up our abode "in Him," it is possible for us to experience Heaven now. We do not have to die to be "in Him"; we can be "in Him" now. When we pass away and enter Heaven, we will be "in Him," but we can be "in Him" now when we are born again and die to self.

This book has developed out of the growth of the relationship between God and myself.

# Chapter 1

# *In the Beginning...*

When I was a young person, I talked with the Lord frequently. We developed a relationship that I believe is the basis of the "in Him" message. *Being in Him is a relationship, not a position.* It is knowing who we are, knowing who He is, and knowing that we have a communion, a union, and a fellowship with Him that carries into every realm of our lives. When the realization settles in that we are in Him and that He is in us, suddenly our prayers take on special meaning. We pray in a different way. Because He is with us all the time and we are with Him all the time, we do more than just set aside time to pray (although that is an important part).

We pray all the time, any time—in season and out of season, when we are alone and when we are with others. Location, time, and surroundings do not make any difference. We find that we do not need to set aside specific time to pray and study because our lives are filled with Him. He overshadows everything that we do. As a result, life takes on greater meaning. We become more willing to do for Him. We walk a new walk because of our change of heart.

We have been taught that we must pray for a certain number of hours, study so many hours, and go to church so many times. We are told that we must meet all these requirements to make ourselves worthy enough to talk to Him or to hear from Him. This message of being "in Him" set me free; it helped me to see that I am what I am by the will of God. I am not what I am because I made myself this way, I prayed myself this way, or I studied myself to this place. I am what I am by the will of God. I am what I am because He lives inside me, because I live inside Him, and because we have a communion with one another.

### He Draws Us

*No man can come to Me, except the Father which hath sent Me draw him: and I will raise him up at the last day* (John 6:44).

Whenever we feel drawn to the Lord Jesus Christ, wanting to know Him better, we must recognize that it is God's desire to draw us to Himself. When the Father draws us to Him and we become close to Him, we are rekindling a relationship that was already established in Heaven. Jesus said it in His Word; we come to Him because He draws us to Himself. Jesus is always drawing us to Himself. I tell people who say they want their husbands saved that the Father wants their husbands saved more than they do. The Father wants our sons or daughters or grandchildren or our relatives, or the person we work with saved and brought to the fullness of God more than we do. Jesus is drawing people to Himself.

I came to know who the "in Him" was when I decided to pursue Him. He became more real to me and made "in Him" more real to me. The closer I came to Him, the more He drew me to Himself. It was like a full agreement. The more I wanted to find out about "in Him," the more He poured into me and allowed me to understand. As I started to walk toward Him, it seemed that He began to run toward me.

### Deception

The importance of understanding what being in Him was became more real to me. The Lord wanted me to know Him because He wanted me to teach others about "in Him." The "in Him" message is vitally important because when we know who we are in Christ, we are not deceived. Deception comes when people do not know who they are. Consider a tiny baby who is kidnapped from his mother in the hospital. That child could grow up thinking the kidnapper is his mother. The baby can be deceived. A three-year-old who has been kidnapped would have an adjustment time, but eventually he could be deceived to believe this person is his mother. But, as an adult, no one can convince me that I am not Bernita Fulton Conway. I know that my dad is my dad and my mom is my mom. There is no possible way to deceive me in that, because I grew up knowing both my father and mother.

In the same respect, take a person who is a baby in Christ. That person can be deceived. Yet it is very difficult for a person who knows who he (or she) is, who his Father God is, who his brother Jesus is, and who the Holy Spirit is to be deceived. Such a person cannot be convinced that he is anyone other than who he really is—a child of God.

The word *deception* means wandering or leading astray. People will not wander from God Himself when they know who they are in Christ. Immediately, the Father in them, the Jesus in them, the Spirit in them (because they are all one in the same Spirit), will draw them back.

## The Mystery Revealed

*Even the mystery which hath been hid from ages and from generations, but now is made manifest to His saints: to whom God would make known what is the riches of the glory of this mystery among the Gentiles; which is Christ in you, the hope of glory* (Colossians 1:26-27).

When we know who we are and whose we are, the possibility for deception will be very slim. That is why the "in Him" message is so important today. It is the mystery revealed, the mystery of the *ascended life*. A mystery is a secret that is out of range of our unassisted natural apprehension. It is only by divine revelation that it can come to us. A mystery is also made known by God in a manner and time appointed by God. This is the true mystery, which is *Christ in you, the hope of glory.*

*Whom we preach, warning every man, and teaching every man in all wisdom; that we may present every man perfect in Christ Jesus: whereunto I also labour, striving according to His working, which worketh in me mightily* (Colossians 1:28-29).

When *Christ in you, the hope of glory* is preached, warning every man, teaching every man in all wisdom, it will present every man perfect, mature, and full grown in Christ Jesus and less able to be deceived. It is not totally impossible, but usually very difficult, to deceive someone who has been brought up, built up in Christ, matured, and been made to know who *Christ in you, the hope of glory* is.

Our lives will change as we build ourselves up "in Him" and learn who Christ is in us as the hope of glory. Suddenly, we will be able to fulfill the call that is on our lives, the position to which God has brought us, and the place that He has put us into perfectly, because we will be trained and matured in Him.

When we are in Him and surrounded by the glory, we are healed, we have direction, and we are at peace. We have confidence about where we are headed, where God is taking us, and where we are going with Him. When we are in Him, we are in the will of God. When we are in the will of God, we find ourselves desiring His presence.

### Testimony

While I was searching for the Lord and His plan for my life, my husband Jerry and I went to Florida. We attended a meeting at a church in Florida. I was very, very troubled in my spirit, and I needed ministry. I thought that I would go to a specific church and that God would meet me there. We went to the church, and I felt that what I needed was a gentle touch from the Lord. However, the meeting took an abrupt turn, and it ended up as a deliverance service. It was a wild, wild service. Those attending the service went to the front for prayer, and the ministers went down the line praying over them.

I thought, *No, Lord. I said that I would come and meet You here. I asked You to give me the peace and the gentleness that I need—exactly what I need to get through this time in my life.*

I walked up front, and the whole front of the big church was filled. The ministers were coming down the line, laying hands on people, casting devils out. I thought, *Lord, if I need deliverance to find peace, here I am.* The minister progressed through the line in my direction in his deliverance mode, but when he approached me, he abruptly stopped. He took my hands, looked me in the eyes, and said, "God has told me that you are to read Ephesians 1, 2, and 3; Philippians 1, 2, and 3; and Colossians 1, 2, and 3. You will find your answer in those books and in those chapters."

I left the meeting thinking, *That does not sound like what I was looking for*, but I began to read Ephesians 1–3, Philippians 1–3, and Colossians 1–3. These chapters became the truth, the basis, and the foundation for the entire "in Him" message.

## "In Him" in Ephesians 1

Read through Ephesians 1. Circle, underline, or note in some distinguishing fashion each time the following phrases occur: "in Christ," "in Him," "in whom," "in Jesus," "of Him," "by Him," and "through Him." It is amazing how many times the various "in Him" references are used.

*Paul, an apostle of Jesus Christ by the will of God, to the saints which are at Ephesus, and to the faithful in Christ Jesus: Grace be to you, and peace, from God our Father, and from the Lord Jesus Christ. Blessed be the God and Father of our Lord Jesus Christ, who hath blessed us with all spiritual blessings in heavenly places in Christ: according as He hath chosen us in Him before the foundation of the world, that we should be holy and without blame before Him in love: having predestinated us unto the adoption of children by Jesus Christ to Himself, according to the good pleasure of His will* (Ephesians 1:1-5).

If we want to find blessings, spiritual blessings, we will find them in heavenly places, but they will be in Christ. It is His will that we have all things, whatsoever we need. We have been *predestinated*, which means that before anything else was, He had a plan for our lives. When we were not even a thought or sparkle in our fathers' or mothers' eyes, we were with Him. We were with God in the spirit realm until He placed us on this earth in these bodies He chose for us, and then He brought us back to Himself through the adoption of children.

*To the praise of the glory of His grace, wherein He hath made us accepted in the beloved. In whom we have redemption through His blood, the forgiveness of sins, according to the riches of His grace* (Ephesians 1:6-7).

Once grace begins to be poured out on us, He is going to make us accepted in the beloved. He is going to do it for us. That is grace.

*Having made known unto us the mystery of His will, according to His good pleasure which He hath purposed in Himself* (Ephesians 1:9).

He previously decided and brought it forth in a revelation of divine mystery so that we would be able to understand who He is, who we are, and how we can be in Him.

God previously planned it. We are gifts to God. He gave us our salvation as a gift, and the result is that we are a gift back to God. He created in us, through Christ Jesus, by the Holy Spirit, the gift of salvation. He gave us that gift. But, now, we are gifts back to Him, and He designed it that way.

*In whom ye also trusted, after that ye heard the word of truth, the gospel of your salvation: in whom also after that ye believed, ye were sealed with that holy Spirit of promise, which is the earnest of our inheritance until the redemption of the purchased possession, unto the praise of His glory* (Ephesians 1:13-14).

After we trusted in Him, after we heard the word of truth and believed the gospel of salvation, we believed it in our hearts and spoke it with our mouths. After we believed in Him, we were sealed with the Holy Spirit of promise. He sealed us with the Holy Spirit, literally, filling up any cracks in our faith. He did this so that we could know who we are, know who He is, and know that we could have this walk with Him. He wanted us to know that we could proceed through this life and that He would be waiting at the other end, saying, "Come on. Come and see Me, now."

### Heavenly Realms

In the Epistles, Paul said that he had met with Christ. He met with Him in Heaven, yet he did not know if he had met Him in the body or out of the body (see 2 Cor. 12:2-3). In addition, Paul said Christ is seated in heavenly places and that we can be there too (see Eph. 1:3,20). Paul heard this message directly from Jesus Christ. It is a direct revelation of the mystery of Jesus Himself. Jesus is our way into the heavenly realms. There is a position for us with Him in the heavenly realm, and we can be there and be with Him, now.

We can grow in Him, but we cannot be seated in heavenly places until we go through the cross and are crucified with Him. If we want to become more like Him, if we want to know Him better, if we want to know more about Christ, then we must die to the desires of this earthly body. As we die to our earthly wisdom and abilities and realize that we have no ability and no wisdom, then all His ability and wisdom are made available to us. We must acknowledge that, in and of ourselves, we have no strength, yet we may have all strength through Him (see Phil 4:13).

Allowing ourselves to be crucified prepares us to be elevated to the heavenlies, to meet with Him, to sit with Him, to hear from Him. From this position we may receive the very ways of God. We may know His will, and we may take on His character. As the work of the cross becomes completed in us, our relationship with Christ is enriched.

# Chapter 2

# *Sin*

The Holy Spirit is the Advocate. The wonderful thing about the Holy Spirit is that He is the one who draws us to Christ. That is His purpose—to draw sinners to Christ and to draw believers who have turned away from Christ back to Him. The Holy Spirit, the Advocate, can help us to overcome in any area of sin.

## Testimony

I will never forget the time in my life when I felt completely beaten down and frustrated, yet I kept seeking the Lord. He kept saying, "Do not stop walking toward Me. Keep coming toward Me." We must never allow unbelief to prevent us from going forward. The most important thing I needed to do in my life was to continue to walk toward Him no matter what I did, no matter what I said, no matter what I felt.

## David and Bathsheba

After David committed adultery with Bathsheba, she became pregnant and had a child. A prophet came to David and told him that his child would die. Upon hearing this news, David put on his fasting clothes, entered the sanctuary, and began to pray. He prayed and sought God regarding the child. David did not eat or drink anything. He stayed in the sanctuary. Finally, David noticed that the people at the side were whispering, so he asked them if his son was dead. When they told David that the boy had died, he got up, took off his fasting clothes, washed himself, and had something to eat. David's servants had been concerned how he would respond to the news and were amazed at his actions. They had expected him to be distraught. Yet when they asked for an explanation, he responded, "I needed to repent. I did so, but now that there is nothing to be repentant over, I am ready to go on." (See Second Samuel 11–12.)

We need to follow David's example concerning going on with God after personal repentance. We have to ask ourselves if we have failed or done wrong. If so, we must ask God to forgive us. Then we must put on our clothes, wash ourselves, and walk with God instead of staying in the sin or in the weakness.

## Peter

*And saw two ships standing by the lake: but the fishermen were gone out of them, and were washing their nets. And He entered into one of the ships, which was Simon's, and prayed him that he would thrust out a little from the land. And He sat down, and taught the people out of the ship. Now when He had left speaking, He said unto Simon, Launch out into the deep, and let down your nets for a draught. And Simon answering said unto Him, Master, we have toiled all the night, and have taken nothing: nevertheless at Thy word I will let down the net. And when they had this done, they enclosed a great multitude of fishes: and their net brake. And they beckoned unto their partners, which were in the other ship, that they should come and help them. And they came, and filled both the ships, so that they began to sink. When Simon Peter saw it, he fell down at Jesus' knees, saying, Depart from me; for I am a sinful man, O Lord* (Luke 5:2-8).

Was there anywhere in the text where Peter got into any kind of sin? Was there any adultery? Had he been fornicating, lying, stealing, murdering, cheating, or doing wrong things to his parents? Had he been breaking any of the Ten Commandments? *No!* He was doing one thing: He was being disobedient. He was disobedient to the word of the Lord. The Lord had told him to push out into the deep and put down his nets. But he said, "No, all I want is one net."

Peter recognized his disobedience. He said, "My God, You have to get away from me. I cannot stand it because I am a sinful man." But his sin was not from the list of sins with which we typically label people; his sin was unbelief, disobedience, and an inability to see the whole picture. That is why he told Jesus that he couldn't take His presence. Peter was close to Christ and saw how pure He was, how perfect He was, and how clean He was. In contrast, Peter recognized how dark and dreary and empty he was because he could not see the whole picture. He responded, "Get away from me, Lord, for I am a sinful man." Peter recognized the sin in his life and was convicted.

## Man at the Pool of Bethesda

Another sin situation involved the man with the infirm spirit. He had laid at the pool of Bethesda for *38 years*. His friends or relatives had to carry him there and then carry him away day after day throughout that entire time. He was waiting for the movement of the water so that he might be healed. Then Jesus came along and saw the man's need. He told him to be made whole, to take up his bed, and to walk. As the man left, Jesus told him to go and sin no more. What was the man's sin for 38 years? This was a man who was carried to and from the pool, an infirm man who had laid on a mat all day. What could his sin have been? How could we charge this man with a particular sin? His sin was unbelief. He did not believe that he could be healed. Yet he had to believe to receive all that God had for him. (See John 5:1-16.)

## Sin Hinders Fullness

It is important to understand how sin keeps us from the fullness of the "in Him" message, for it is a message of Christ in you, the hope of glory. The reason people are in the world and not born again is because they do not believe. It is not because they have

sinned great sins. No matter how many sins an unbeliever has committed, hell does not become any deeper.
Unbelievers are unbelievers. Christians are the ones
who have to deal with and be concerned with sin. An
unbeliever is a person who does not believe in Jesus
Christ. Once a person comes to believe in Jesus Christ,
then he or she must address the sin of failing to do the
will of God.

The sins of unbelief and disobedience cause us to
have no peace. Rebellion and disobedience are the
areas that cause us to have many problems inside ourselves. There are many sins that God hates that cause
us to know that we are in rebellion and disobedience
against God. These sins include pride, self-righteous-
ness, self-centeredness, self-pity, self-punishment, and
attitudes like "I deserve it" or "I'll control others." All
these sins stem from unbelief.

When Scripture records Peter asking the Lord to
depart from him because he was a sinful man, it is not
saying that Peter had sinned a great sin. He merely saw
how clean Jesus was and how dirty he was because of
his unbelief. Unbelief keeps us from true relationship
with Jesus. When we make Jesus the Lord of our lives,
we begin to learn to turn away from unbelief. We start
saying, "Lord, show me what You want me to do. Show
me the direction. Show me how You want me to do it.
Show me when You want me to do it." Then, we wait
for His direction.

Be encouraged. God will let us know what He wants
us to do and when He wants us to do it. All we are
responsible to do is to be obedient at the time. He will

never put on us more than we can handle or more than we have the anointing, understanding, or training to do. He would never ask us to be the head of a church of 2,000 until we were first head over a church of 20. God prepares and equips those whom He calls.

## Sin, a State of Being

Jesus needs to be Lord of our lives. Once He is Lord of our lives, we go into the realm of righteousness. Sin is a state of being, not a state of doing. Before we were born again, we were in the state of sin. We are in sin when we are in the state of unbelief. Righteousness is also a state of being and not a state of doing. We cannot *do* enough good things to please God. We must do what He asks us to do, not what we tell Him we are going to do. It pleases God when we do what He asks us to do and do it well with all our hearts. For us to do what we want to do and say that it pleases God is wrong. All unrighteousness is sin, and our own ideas are not God's righteousness. Only what God has asked us to do can be called righteous.

Unbelief is simple; whatever is not of faith is sin. Unbelief means that we do not believe God's Word will work, that we are in rebellion against the Word of God. When we are in rebellion, fear, or unbelief, we displease God. When we believe that we are children of God, we know we are the righteousness of God (see 1 Jn. 3:10). This pleases Him.

We do not need to look for areas where we have sinned in the past. We must bury the past, crucify the flesh, and recognize that God is calling us to grow up in Him. We do not need to over-analyze and scrutinize the past, but we must deal with it, repent, and proceed in the call that is on our lives.

### Believing and Confessing

*That if thou shalt confess with thy mouth the Lord Jesus, and shalt believe in thine heart that God hath raised Him from the dead, thou shalt be saved* (Romans 10:9).

What is in our hearts is what we eventually speak. After asking Jesus into our hearts and confessing Him with our mouths, we are made the righteousness of God. By confessing and believing and by believing and confessing, the righteousness of God comes upon us. Because Abraham believed, it was accounted to him for righteousness (see Gal. 3:6). We too can be accounted righteous by our faith.

We know that we believe because we had the faith to believe. We need to look upon our hearts and see if there is sin or pride or unrighteousness of any sort. We must then confess these weaknesses before Christ and let Him remove them. When a person is born again, he is to confess Christ. When a Christian sins, he is to confess the specific sin before God. An unbeliever becomes a believer by confessing Jesus Christ as his Lord. Jesus wants us to know that as we love Him and as we grow up in Him, as we get closer to Him, we will become more and more like Him.

### Judgment

*And the spirit of the Lord shall rest upon him, the spirit of wisdom and understanding, the spirit of*

*counsel and might, the spirit of knowledge and of the
fear of the Lord; and shall make him of quick understanding in the fear of the Lord: and he shall not
judge after the sight of his eyes, neither reprove after
the hearing of his ears* (Isaiah 11:2-3).

A common problem among Christians is looking at
the sins of others and making judgments. It is very
important to watch how we judge. Jesus judged, not by
what others told Him, but by His own spirit. He makes
His decisions by looking into our hearts and judging
for Himself.

"Judge not, that ye be not judged" means that we
should not judge men unrighteously or unfairly (Mt.
7:1). We need to stay away from judging. God is the
one who judges. Jesus judges perfectly and righteously. If we see something in a brother or sister that we
know is wrong, we should ask God to reveal it to him
or her.

God judges perfectly, and He knows how to judge
perfectly. The Holy Spirit is the one who convicts our
hearts and shows us our weaknesses. We do not need
to get into self-condemnation, self-punishment, and self-
judgment. When God, through the Holy Spirit, convicts us, we are convicted that we have been in sin.
There is no self in this conviction. God will work with
us perfectly, completely, and totally so that we might be
set free as He brings us to repentance and correction.

### All of God, None of Self

Anyone who is filled with self cannot be filled with
Jesus. Self is the only sin that I know of that God cannot

deal with; for if we are saying, "I will," then He cannot say, "I will." There cannot be two "I will's" in any given situation. It is either the will of God or our will. God wants us to be free from all selfishness, all self-centeredness, and all pride. In any area that we are taking the credit, we must give God the credit. God deserves the glory for every good thing in our lives.

*For men shall be lovers of their own selves, covetous, boasters, proud, blasphemers, disobedient to parents, unthankful, unholy, without natural affection, truce-breakers, false accusers, incontinent, fierce, despisers of those that are good, traitors, heady, highminded, lovers of pleasures more than lovers of God* (2 Timothy 3:2-4).

A blasphemer is a person who says that he is more important than God is. We may try to label our children as "disobedient to parents," yet we must also be obedient to our heavenly Father. We can be disobedient to our heavenly Father as young people can be disobedient to their earthly fathers. One who is "incontinent" experiences excesses and has no control. A person who is "fierce" has "anger," which is one letter from *danger* (if you add "d" to "anger," you will have "danger").

### Summary

If God be for us, who can be against us? Unbelief is sin, and faith is imputed as righteousness. Faith is the substance of things hoped for and the evidence of things not seen (see Heb. 11:1). The following chart compares unbelief with faith. We must choose the side of faith.

| Negative: Unbelief | Positive: Faith |
|---|---|
| Poverty | Prosperity |
| Sickness | Healing |
| Demons | Deliverance |
| Weakness | Strength |
| Hate | Love |
| Nervousness | Peace |
| Fear | Faith |
| Unbelief | Belief |
| Sin | Righteousness |
| Death | Life |

The way we perceive ourselves is who we are, for what we believe is what we will receive. When we believe that these good things, which are listed on the side of faith, are for us, then God will bring them to us.

### Prayer for New Beginning

If you have not made Jesus the Lord of your life, I want to take a moment to make sure you know Jesus Christ as your Savior and Lord. To receive Jesus Christ as your Savior and Lord, you must confess Him to the glory of God. Pray the following prayer:

*"Jesus, come into my life. Take control of my life. You control my life. I do not know how to control my life. I believe that You know more than I do, and I want You to take care of my life. Come into my heart and be my Lord and Savior."*

If you prayed this prayer, you will be ready for the following chapters of the book. They will build on the foundation that we laid in this chapter by taking you into knowing who you are in Christ, helping you to understand the character of God, and showing how righteousness brings you to the total reality of who God is and what He can do for you.

*"Father, I thank You that the power of God is moving right now. I ask that all who read this book would grow in Your grace and power. I thank You, Lord, that the peace of God rules and abides with these readers that they might know that Jesus Christ is Lord to the glory of God. I thank You that the power of God is in our giving way to Him, in believing and in receiving. Thank You that we are now made the righteousness of God in Christ because we have made Jesus Christ the Lord of our lives. I pray a blessing on every person, and I ask You to be present with us as we go forward in our lives. Amen."*

# Chapter 3

# *Character of God*

To come closer to God and to understand Him and the "in Him" message, we must learn about His character. Once we discover what He is like, we can understand how to become closer to Him and be in Him.

*And thou shalt love the Lord thy God with all thine heart, and with all thy soul, and with all thy might* (Deuteronomy 6:5).

Each Israelite family would place what was called a *mezuzah* on their doorways that contained this Scripture verse. They would touch their hand to the *mezuzah*, touch their hand to their lips, and then back to the *mezuzah* because these were words God told them to put in their hearts and write on their doorposts (see Deut. 6:6,9). Many Jewish people put these *mezuzahs* on the side of their doorways yet today, and when they go through their doors they lay their hands on them. This is to let the Lord know that they love

Him, that they know who He is, and that they want to be more like Him.

## Love

To develop the character of God in our lives, we need to know who He is and what He is like. The love of God is one of the most powerful aspects of His character. As we love Him and His children with the love He has given to us, He responds to us with love.

## Jesus

*In the beginning was the Word, and the Word was with God, and the Word was God* (John 1:1).

Jesus exemplified the character of His Father throughout His life on earth. Whenever a child is born, he is born to be like his parents. He may have the same color of eyes as his parents. He may have the same color of hair or the same body stance. Different traits of a child will reflect the characteristics of his parents. This happens to both males and females; they inherit the character of their parents. Jesus Christ, the Son, definitely took on the full character of God. When we take Jesus Christ into our hearts, we too have the full character of God available to us and need to demonstrate it to the world.

## Testimony

When we lived in Ohio, I had a friend whose husband was killed when her son was a year and a half old. Her husband was a farmer and spent a lot of time in the fields. As a result, the son never spent much time with the father. Due to his father's death, he never got to know his father during his later formative years. However, when the young man approached 16 or 17 years of age, his mother was amazed. Her son began to walk exactly like his father, talk exactly like his father, use the same inflections in his voice, and even look exactly like his father. She found it a bit frightening because it seemed as though her husband had come back to life in his son. This son was never familiar enough with his father to mimic him. He had never really had the opportunity to see his father model these traits. He became like his father just because he was his son.

Jesus knew the Father. He said, "I know the Father and the Father knows Me" (see Jn. 10:15). They had a tremendous relationship, and Jesus became just like His Father. We know today that we have the ability to become like God through Jesus Christ.

*But as many as received Him, to them gave He power to become the sons of God, even to them that believe on His name* (John 1:12).

When we receive Christ, He gives us the ability to become like God, to receive the character of God, to become a son of God. We are His representatives on this earth so that we might exemplify and show others the true character of God. We demonstrate God's character through our lives, in the way we live, in the way we talk, and in the way we carry ourselves. When we receive Jesus Christ, He gives us the power to become sons of God. This does not refer to those who are born the regular way through the will of man or the will of the flesh; it refers to those who are born of God as a result of His will and His grace.

## Holy Spirit

Another way the character of God is revealed to us is by and through the Spirit of God. The Spirit of God always brings glory to the Father. He will never bring a reproach against the Father in any way. The Holy Spirit is so holy; He wants to protect God's name and character. Therefore, the Holy Spirit labors to bring situations to the place where God receives glory and praise and is exalted in the minds and hearts of people. The Holy Spirit orchestrates our lives to bring glory to God. He often takes a negative situation and turns it around for His name's sake, that the character of God may never be marred in our lives.

It is terribly wrong to judge one another, for in doing so, we are judging the character of a child of God. We do not have that right. God says, "This is My beloved Son in whom I am well pleased" (see Mt. 3:17). Therefore, we have to recognize the character of God in one another. We are called to love each other in the spiritual realm. It is the character of God in a person that we love.

Each of us responds uniquely to God. We do not have to be like anyone else. We should appreciate and love each other in our differences. We each have a unique place in this Body, and it is a place that God has fashioned for us. We have aspects of His character that no one else has. If we do not let Him be Him through us, then part of God's character is not being expressed.

> *But rise, and stand upon thy feet: for I have appeared unto thee for this purpose, to make thee a minister and a witness both of these things which thou hast seen, and of those things in the which I will appear unto thee* (Acts 26:16).

The character of God is revealed to us for a purpose, just as it was to Paul in the above Scripture. Jesus personally presented the full character of God to Paul. He came to him in revelation form and showed him the character of God so that Paul might open the blind eyes, turn them from darkness to light, and turn them from the power of satan unto God that they might receive forgiveness of sins (see Acts 26:18). That was the purpose of Paul's life. When he met Christ, he began to see the whole character of God and to know the purpose of God. Today, the Epistles of Paul beautifully reveal God and His character to us in order to help us fulfill our purposes in Him.

### God's Will

> *If ye be willing and obedient, ye shall eat the good of the land* (Isaiah 1:19).

God's character is revealed to us by His will. The will of God is His way, and His way is His will. He wants us to choose to do His will. There are areas in our lives in which we must yield our wills and become obedient to God's will. When we do so, we will eat "the good of the land." As we yield our wills to His will, He brings us to a new level of relationship with Him.

God expresses His character through the anointing that He places in our lives. He uses each one of us in a unique way in the Body of Christ. Through His anointing, His character is brought out in us, and we are able to impact many lives.

## Testimony

In one day, two people complimented me by acknowledging seemingly opposite attributes. I had one person tell me, "You are so strong. I have never met someone as strong as you." Another said, "I have never met anyone as meek and as quiet as you." One said I was so forceful, and the other said I was as meek as a lamb. Since these were such extreme concepts, I wondered which I was. Then I realized that the aspect of the character of God that each of these persons needed to see was what they saw in me. They were not seeing me in either case; they were witnessing the character of God through my life as He desired to reveal Himself to them. Through this experience, I learned that each of us has a unique call to express a dimension of the character of God in the earth. God has entrusted us with part of His character, and we are anointed to fulfill His purposes.

## Jeremiah

*Then said I [Jeremiah], Ah, Lord God! behold, I cannot speak: for I am a child. But the Lord said unto me, Say not, I am a child: for thou shalt go to all that*

*I shall send thee, and whatsoever I command thee thou shalt speak* (Jeremiah 1:6-7).

Jeremiah began to enter into the full character of God from the very beginning of his walk. God began to speak to him, and he began to know God. The Lord sanctified Jeremiah. He covered him with grace and ordained him. It is said that Jeremiah became a prophet at about age 24, which was unheard of. People of biblical times generally never started any active ministry until they were 30. That explains why God encouraged Jeremiah not to be limited by his youth.

We need to put our excuses for not serving the Lord in the place of Jeremiah's. And in each case, God's response will be like His response to Jeremiah's protest, "Say not...." He is saying to you and me, "Say not, I am a child, I am a woman, I am married, I am single, I am black, I am Hispanic, I am divorced, I am too little, or I am too weak." God is asking us to give Him our hearts, our mouths, our lives. When we do, He will speak through us. He reprimanded Jeremiah, telling him to say not that he was a child. God reprimands us in the same way, but God will also guide us, just as He did Jeremiah. God will send us where we need to go, and He will give us what to speak when we need Him to do so. We do not have to fear, saying, "I do not know what to say." The Lord said He will deliver us and give us what to say.

God encouraged Jeremiah, telling him, "If you will work with Me, I will work with you. I will give you all My character, all My ability. If you will let Me, I will do the work. The Word is active. It is the rod of authority, of discipline, of chastisement." God was willing to work with Jeremiah to make him successful in fulfilling the work He had called him to accomplish. God did the same with Paul as He did with Jeremiah: He set each of His servants on his feet and instructed him to go and do the job before him.

### Forgiveness

Forgiveness is an aspect of the character of God. A key aspect of forgiveness is learning to forgive ourselves. Once we have asked for and received God's forgiveness, we must forgive ourselves. We also must forgive others. At times we can find it too difficult to forgive in our own strength, but God will forgive through us because His character, which is being formed in us, is forgiveness. Jesus personified forgiveness as He hung on the cross and asked God to forgive His accusers rather than condemn them. We too are called to walk in forgiveness.

### Compassion

We need to take on the character of God's compassion. He asks us to love as He loved—unconditionally. His love is not physical or mere emotional love, but it is a love with depth that stirs the very essence of man. When we are moved with compassion, it causes us to *do*. We become motivated with His passion. Only God can love with such impact, but we can love this way too when we are in Him.

### Wisdom

God's character is revealed in His wisdom, and it is this wisdom that He reveals to His children. A person with God's wisdom is a person who is skillful, mature, ready to teach. When we walk in wisdom, we soar above our circumstances. Circumstances do not control the one who walks in wisdom; rather, he controls the circumstances.

Wisdom is being able to know what to do before we are faced with a situation. We trust God that when a need arises He will come to us by the Spirit of wisdom and bring our answer. That is the wisdom of God. As we walk in wisdom, we will see His character being formed in us, shaping our character.

## Righteousness

When we know who we are, we have arrived at righteousness. We know that we are justified. It says in Ephesians that when we accept Jesus Christ, He plants in us a deposit, a down payment, of the Holy Spirit. We have *equity* built up in us because God has sown equity within us. The Holy Spirit is our equity. After He comes to indwell us, His presence begins to grow. The more of our minds and our spirits and our bodies that we allow Him to have, the more His character begins to flood our minds, spirits, and bodies. We must actively pursue God, His Word, and His ways in order to arrive at this position of righteousness.

## Grace

*And of His fulness have all we received, and grace for grace* (John 1:16).

Grace is the house where wisdom, love, righteousness, and faith live. Grace is a far-reaching dimension

*Bernita J. Conway*

of the character of God. He is full of grace. Once we receive Jesus Christ as our personal Lord and Savior, we go from grace to grace to grace. In any situation we face, if we ask God for grace, He will grant it. We cannot work to receive God's grace; it is a gift, manifested in us through Jesus Christ.

## Fullness of the Godhead

*For in Him dwelleth all the fulness of the Godhead bodily. And ye are complete in Him, which is the head of all principality and power* (Colossians 2:9-10).

When we accepted Jesus Christ as our Lord and Savior, God sent Him into our hearts. God will not let go of our lives because He has made a deposit inside us—His Son, Jesus Christ. For God to reject us, He would also be rejecting His Son and His own character because He planted the fullness of Himself in us when He gave us Jesus. It pleased the Father to fill us with Himself, and He desires that we recognize His character and come into the fullness He has prepared. When we came to Him, we received the power and the abilities of God and were challenged to want more of God's character. Christ exemplified God's character on this earth.

## Seeds

God wants us to be trees of righteousness. We receive the seed of God, His character, in our hearts, and then we begin to plant that seed in others. Many welcome the seed, desiring the full character of God to be planted in them. These persons will grow and also become trees of righteousness. As trees produce fruit, nuts, and seeds, so trees of righteousness produce after themselves, including a variety of outpourings of God's character.

When an acorn drops from an oak tree, it begins to put roots into the ground and sprouts, and the result is always going to be an oak tree. Whatever seed goes in the ground, it will always produce after its own kind. The seed of God is what has been planted in us; therefore, the seed, the character of God, is what we produce. When we have the seed of God, it increases our desire to be like Jesus. We will act like God, emulating Jesus, wanting to take on His character. Other people will notice the character of God being expressed in our lives.

## Joshua

Joshua was a man in the Bible who definitely had a purpose, and God fulfilled that purpose in his life. Joshua wanted people to become more like God. His heartfelt desire was that God would be glorified by the lives of His people. Joshua constantly worked with the children of Israel, leading them to become more like God, to see as He saw, and to live in the victory He prepared for them. When the people refused to walk in the character of God, Joshua was hurt by their attitudes.

When the children of Israel entered the promised land and were given rest, they began to go their separate ways. The Reubenites, Gadites, and the half tribe of Manasseh went across the Jordan River and built a tremendous altar. It was so high that the people could see it from all around. Their brethren on the other side of the river thought they had built it for wrong reasons. They thought that these tribes had gone after other gods. They sent a group of people over to the Reubenites, Gadites, and the half tribe of Manasseh to tell them that they could not build this altar because it was wrong, that it was sin to worship other gods. Upon hearing the accusations against them, they responded, "God knows our hearts, that we wanted this altar to be a witness, not to be a contention between us as tribes" (see Josh. 22:22-28).

People misunderstood why they built the altar, but both sides were right in their hearts. The one wanted to build the altar to be a witness. The other wanted to keep their brothers from heading in the wrong direction. Each party wanted the character of God that was in them to be preserved. They knew it was wrong to go after other gods. Both groups had love in their hearts. Both of them had purpose in their hearts.

## Anger and Encouragement

Anger is part of the character of God that Jesus demonstrated only when He saw the character of God being trampled. Jesus did not allow the character of God to be mistreated. He always wanted the character of God to be highly esteemed.

We must come to the aid of our brothers and sisters in Christ when we see that they are weak in an area of the character of God or that they need lifted up and strengthened. When we see the areas where they need encouraged, we need to help them, guide them, and pray for them. If in their weakness the character of God is being misrepresented, that is the only time we have the right to have righteous indignation toward any of our brothers and sisters in Christ.

When growing in the character of God becomes a priority in our lives, we want to assemble together. We desire to come together with other members of the Body of Christ to implant the character of God in each other, provoking one another to perfection in Him. When we see the character of God in others, we realize that no man is an island and that no man can make it alone. Everyone needs the fellowship and guidance we receive when we gather together with other Christians; it gives us the ability to see the multifaceted character of God in action in one another. We can see areas in other people's lives that are reflections of various aspects of God's character that we may not yet be walking in. As a result, we are challenged to grow and to desire more of Him.

### Being a Witness

*To reveal His Son in me, that I might preach Him among the heathen; immediately I conferred not with flesh and blood* (Galatians 1:16).

"I want Christ revealed in me that I might preach." The whole reason that we need the character of God revealed in us is that we might be witnesses and preach. We need to build up others to become conformable to His character and be made complete in Him. This includes encouraging and strengthening others to be brought to all virtue, all ability, all excellence, all value, all perfection, that they might be victorious over self and sin and fear. That is the expression and fulfillment of the character of God.

Everything we see in Christ, we have the ability to enjoy. When we are rooted and grounded in the Word of God, in the love of God, and in the ability of God, then His character begins to come forth. We start to experience the riches of His glory that are found in His fullness. All His abilities and resources are ours to request.

We progress from glory to glory and from grace to grace in His character. We see that Jesus Christ is all God's character in one person. To receive His character is to be totally transformed. This character is transferable from Jesus to us and from us to others. Therefore, we can become catalysts, stirring others to want the character of God in their lives. When God is number one in our lives, our own desires become less important and being like God becomes our main focus.

*"Father, I thank You for Your character that You make available to us. Lord God, I ask You to transfer into us the very Spirit of Christ, the very character of God, the fullness of the Godhead to dwell in us bodily. I ask that as we go forth daily, hourly, and minute by minute, that You would use us mightily in the Body of Christ to transfer Your character and to share Your very being with others. I pray that we might be so infected and impacted by the seed of God that we would have the revelation of the Lord Jesus Christ in our lives and that through us the very character of God would be translated into the world. Thank You, Lord, for what You have done for us. In Jesus' name, amen."*

# Chapter 4

# *Righteousness*

*Righteousness* is the character or quality of "right being." It is also the position of being in right standing with God, knowing that He is fair with us and always judges us righteously. We never have to worry that God will misjudge us or overreact to our mistakes. He always gives us the right sentence or response, the perfect one for the situation.

### Born of the Flesh, Born of the Spirit

When we come into the state of righteousness, we begin to learn *who* we are, and God begins to work in us to show us *whose* we are. We recognize our position in the family of God and acknowledge that He is our Father.

None of us had anything to do with our physical births. Jesus said to Nicodemus, "You must be born again, not of the flesh, not of the will of man, but of the spirit" (see Jn. 3:3-9). We did not have anything to do with being born. Somebody else had everything to do with bringing us into the world.

It is the same with being born again. We had no part in our born-again experience, except that we believed God. We believed what He had to say was truth. When we received that truth, we were transformed into new beings, new creatures, accepting the righteousness of God. Now, we have His righteousness and not our own righteousness.

## Testimony

I tried for years to live a very noble life, to do everything right, and to do good according to my personal moral system. I worked for many organizations, including the United Way, United Fund, Boy Scouts, and Girl Scouts, thinking I was making points with God by doing these good works. I continued to feel more miserable and tired and frustrated; because at the end of it all, I still considered myself a failure. I was weighed down with many projects and from trying to prove that I was good. I eventually experienced a mental breakdown because of the pressure I was placing on myself to prove that I was acceptable. However, the only thing I really had to do was say, "God, I receive Your Son, Jesus Christ, and in the receiving of Your Son, Jesus Christ, You make me good. Now I do not have to work anymore for Your acceptance. If You tell me to help the United Way, I will. If You tell me to help the Boy Scouts, I will. But, I will work because

You have told me to work, not because I think I have to perform."

## "Rightwiseness"

"*Rightwiseness*" is the way righteousness was spelled many years ago. Rightwiseness is righteousness, and it is part of the character of God. It is consistent with His nature and with His promises. Whatever conforms to the revealed will of God is righteousness. It is the sum total of all the requirements of God. There is nothing left for us to do in order to prove to God that we are good or right or perfect or acceptable for His Kingdom. Once we have believed God and it has been accounted to us as righteousness, we have fulfilled all the requirements God has made of us.

## Testimony

I talked with a tax client, who annually comes to the office and updates us on all the things she has done wrong in the past year. She is such a sweet, bubbly Christian. One day she asked me, "Why does God still love me so much? Why does He care about me? I have done this and this and this. The only thing I have not done is climb Mt. Everest in the sin realm, but yet, God loves me. He protects me. He tells me things for the protection of my family, and He reveals things to me. Why does He do this for me?" I simply looked at her and said, "It is because of His mercy. Because you count yourself as guilty, He agrees with you that you are guilty and mercy is poured on it and you are made free. It is because you are the righteousness of God and He loves you that mercy is poured on you and you are set on a path to perfection." We must believe that His love, which is based on His righteousness and mercy, is His character and that He responds to us from His character and not from our personal worthiness.

## Family Likeness

Once we know who we are, there is no way in the world that we can be talked out of our identity. No one can ever convince me that I am not my father's daughter. I look like him. I act like him in some ways—not in all, but in some. We have a shared likeness. By virtue of being his daughter, I took on his name and some of his characteristics. God does the same for us. When we become born again and become part of His family, we take on His name. He will not take His name away from us because we have been adopted, and adopted children can never be "unadopted." We are made permanent heirs and members of His family.

## Abraham

*And he* [Abram] *believed in the Lord; and He counted it to him for righteousness* (Genesis 15:6).

This is one of the first places in the Bible where it speaks of Abram's (whose name God changed to Abraham) believing God. In this passage of Scripture God was encouraging Abram, promising him a son and numerous seed. It says that Abraham believed in the Lord and that the Lord accounted his faith to him for righteousness. God took his believing and made it into righteousness and justification. God made Abraham a divine leader because he believed God and was convicted of His truthfulness. God elevated him to lead others into the blessings of God—his whole family, his seed, his seed's seed, down to us today and to all those who believe as Abraham did. As the result of our faith, we will inherit Abraham's promises of prosperity, posterity, blessings, justification, and whatever we may need.

Because Abraham believed that what God had to say was the truth, he had a righteous relationship with Him. The faith of Abraham has been transferred to his seed throughout the generations, to all who have dared to believe God as Abraham did. We are seeds of Abraham, sons of Abraham. Abraham's believing made him righteous. He was not made righteous because he did the right things, but because he believed God. He believed and was made righteous.

Our righteousness is based on our faith—our faith in the Lord Jesus Christ and our position in Him. Exercising this faith brings the soul into a vital union with God in Christ, and inevitably, it will produce righteousness. Righteousness breeds conformity to the will of God, which brings forth the fruits of righteousness.

When we accepted righteousness, right standing with God and right being with God, we received by faith like Abraham did. It was conviction. Faith is the conviction of God's truthfulness. We are totally convicted and convinced that God is truthful and whatever He said is truth. If He said it, it is right and it is truth. When we hear His voice instructing us in our inner man, we must be convinced of the depth and truth of that word, just as we are convicted of the truthfulness of the written Word.

## Authority

Once we are born again, having accepted Jesus Christ as our Savior, we are owned by God our Father, and Jesus Christ is our brother. We prayed, believed, and accepted Him based upon our conviction of God's truthfulness, upon our belief that what He said was truth. We never again have to convince anyone, including ourselves, that we are changed. We know that we have a relationship with Jesus Christ.

When we walk in righteousness, we have authority by position, which is in Christ. The position that we hold in Him causes us to have authority because of *whose* we are, not who we are. This leaves no place for pride because we have done nothing to earn this position.

Our position in God gives us authority over satan. We have authority over sickness; therefore, we can believe Him for healing. We can believe God for answers to prayers regarding our family, regarding our household, regarding the ministry, etc. We trust His ability. He has built in us ownership and equity. He owns our lives, not just our physical lives, but our whole state of being.

## Connected to the Vine

*I am the true vine, and My Father is the husband-man. Every branch in Me that beareth not fruit He*

*taketh away: and every branch that beareth fruit, He*
*purgeth it, that it may bring forth more fruit* (John
15:1-2).

As we are connected to Christ by righteousness, in
righteousness, and through righteousness, He brings
forth answers to the needs that we have in our lives.
He brings forth healing and financial blessings. He
brings forth whatever "fruit" it is that will meet our
need.

It is important to note, however, that the vine does
not bring forth the fruit. The branches bring forth
fruit. When we are united with the vine, which is Christ,
we bring forth fruit. We bring forth a harvest, the seeds
of which are planted back into the earth and will bring
forth new growth and an even greater harvest.

Any branch that is properly connected to the vine
will bring forth much fruit. The people who have been
born of righteousness and born of Him will begin to
act like Him. The fruit that is in their lives will bring
forth signs of righteousness.

### The Lord Our Righteousness

When we become as a child and receive Jesus, we
are born again and take on His righteousness. It is
because He makes us righteous that we can do righteousness, and we recognize that he who does righteousness is righteous, even as the One who saved us
is righteous.

*In His days Judah shall be saved, and Israel shall*
*dwell safely: and this is His name whereby He shall be*

*called, THE LORD OUR RIGHTEOUSNESS* (Jeremiah 23:6).

One of God's names is *Jehovah Tsid'kenue*, which means "the Lord our righteousness." When we come together with Christ, we begin to act like Him. We begin to talk like Him. Fruit and anointing flow through us as the nature of God is formed in us and we become perfected through Him.

### Testimony

I visited the mental ward in a Parkersburg, West Virginia, hospital. I went into the ward and noticed a woman seated in a wheelchair. I did not pray with every person who was in the mental ward, but this woman stood out. She was seated in the wheelchair crying constantly, just crying and crying and crying. That is why they had her in the mental ward. She could not gain control of her emotions.

I went over to her and asked her permission to lay hands on her. She said, "Yes! Yes! I want you to do that." I laid hands on her and immediately commanded the demon to go. She jumped out of the wheelchair and yelled, "It's gone! It's gone!" All the depression was completely gone! A speech impediment she had since birth was also healed. She immediately stopped crying, but she sat down in the wheelchair and would not get back up again.

She had the faith in God to believe for deliverance from depression and to be healed of a speech impediment, but she could not accept the miracle of being set free from the wheelchair. Her faith/righteousness level was limited, and she received all that she could accept. At that point, I had to leave her in the wheelchair, but she was free of the demons and healed of the speech impediment.

The righteous are those who accept Jesus Christ and accept His plan. They get vitally united with the vine, and all the power that comes with being connected to Him begins to flow through them. As a result, healing and miracles will begin to take place.

## All of God, None of Self

One of the most profound statements I ever heard is, "When we have all of self, we have none of God. When we have some of self, we have some of God. But when we empty ourselves of our righteousness and have none of self, then we can have all of God." It is through humility, through putting aside self, that we become channels of the power of God and His righteousness.

Isaiah 53 sheds light on the progression of righteousness in Jesus' life. He was like a root out of dry ground. He had no form or comeliness. He was despised and humbled of men. Not only was He humbled of men, but He humbled Himself before God, saying, "Not My will, but Thine, be done" (Lk. 22:42). Jesus constantly yielded Himself to the Father. It did not please the Father to see Jesus die, nor to see Him have all our sin and all our sickness upon Him. What did please God, however, was His humility, brokenness, and emptiness.

Jesus had "none of self and all of God." That is what pleased God. It did not please Him to see Jesus go through pain. That idea always bothered me until I realized that it was His humility and submission that pleased God. True righteousness is humility. True righteousness is in knowing that we are God's children and that God in us is the hope of glory.

## Ownership

An unusual rendering for the word *righteousness* is *equity*. Equity is ownership. The part of us we have allowed God to own is His equity. We need to be as Jesus was, for He was a humble man. Jesus' humility through His death on the cross pleased God. Now, our humility in accepting the cross and the depth of its purpose pleases God. When we come before God, we must deal with the pride and self in our lives. Allowing ourselves to be crucified by dying to self makes the way for more equity to be built.

There are many Christians today asking, "Why am I not healed?" I believe that one of the keys to healing is a change of ownership. When we become the righteousness of God in Christ, we are not our own; we belong to Him. We do not own ourselves anymore. We must seek God for what is rightfully ours because of what Jesus accomplished on the cross.

## "In"

The word *in* means a fixed position, as "in Christ" or "in righteousness." To be "in Christ" refers to the relationship of rest; once something is "in," as "in the cup," it is in the cup. It is resting in the cup. When we are in Christ, we are like a liquid that is poured in a glass and rests there. We will find rest for our souls in Christ.

*In* means "all together," none on the outside. It means "in." It means the fullness of the Godhead dwelling in us bodily. Another explanation of the word *in* is something we give ourselves wholly to.

*And the Lord God formed man of the dust of the ground, and breathed into his nostrils the breath of life; and man became a living soul* (Genesis 2:7).

### "Be"

To *be* means to exist, to become, to be as the one compared to. The word *be* also means "breath." It signifies origin. It means to "be" fruitful. In other words, it means to exist fruitfully. The word *be* means to exist. It means I AM. In Exodus 3:14, God essentially said to Moses, "I will be whatever you need Me to be. I AM is sending you."

In Genesis 2:7, "God breathed" is the word *be*. God breathed into; He poured into Adam. He poured into his nostrils the breath of life, His own being, and Adam became a living soul. Adam took on the life of God through the breath of God. Adam exemplifies the statement that our righteousness comes as a result of being in Him. When we are in Him, we have taken on the righteousness of God in Christ.

Second Corinthians 5:17-21 deals with our being in Christ. We have already noted that *be* means "to exist" and *in* means "a fixed position." *If any man "be in Christ,"* if he will exist in a fixed position in Christ, he is a new creature. That means all sickness and disease in our physical bodies and all the wrong patterns of thought are passed away, and all things have become new and of God.

God is righteousness. Christ exemplifies righteousness. We receive the righteousness of God by accepting Jesus Christ and His finished work. When we are in Him, we accept Jesus Christ as our righteousness. *Seek first the Kingdom of God and His righteousness, and "all these things shall be added unto you"* (Mt. 6:33). Righteousness is a position. Righteousness is a being.

The Lord gave me the following prayer/confession regarding righteousness:

> *"I am the righteousness of God in Christ; therefore, I live and move and have my being in Him. When I was made righteous, I became the property of Jesus Christ, and I am not my own person. I am part of God, and He is part of me. All His fullness dwells in me, and I can do all things through Christ who strengthens me. God does not look on my outward man, but He looks on my inward man. As I am renewed day by day, I am cleansed by the power of the Holy Spirit, by the blood, and by the washing of the water of the Word. I am considered washed clean, protected, healed of all physical weakness, and made new in my thought life. I am being renewed day by day, and my spirit man is growing to be just like Jesus—perfect! Amen."*

# Chapter 5

# *Lawbreakers*

### *"Living by the Spirit, Not by the Law"*

*For God so greatly loved and dearly prized the world that He [even] gave up His only begotten (unique) Son, so that whoever believes in (trusts in, clings to, relies on) Him shall not perish (come to destruction, be lost) but have eternal (everlasting) life. For God did not send the Son into the world in order to judge (to reject, to condemn, to pass sentence on) the world, but that the world might find salvation and be made safe and sound through Him. He who believes in Him [who clings to, trusts in, relies on Him] is not judged [he who trusts in Him never comes up for judgment; for him there is no rejection, no condemnation—he incurs no damnation]; but he who does not believe (cleave to, rely on, trust in Him) is judged already... because he has not believed in and trusted in the*

*name of the only begotten Son of God...* ( John 3:16-18
AMP).

We all know that John 3:16 deals with eternal life,
but verses 17 and 18 go deeper into the message. The
crux of Scripture is whether we believe in Jesus Christ
or whether we do not believe in Jesus Christ. Believing
in Jesus Christ gives us the right to walk in the Spirit,
including walking in righteousness, peace, joy, wisdom, redemption, salvation, mercy, grace, and healing. When we believe, we have every grace available to
walk not after the flesh, but after the person of Jesus
Christ.

## Walking in the Spirit

By accepting the sacrifice of Jesus Christ, who sac-
rificed His life on the cross for us, we overcome sin
and deprive it of any power over us in our lives. When
we receive Jesus Christ as our Savior and Lord, we also
receive the Holy Spirit. Unholy desires that have
plagued us in the past become less and less trouble-
some. Consequently, we will not be breaking any law.
We begin to walk in the law of the Spirit. We are walking in the Spirit's way and the Spirit's plan; therefore,
our bodies have to take a backseat, because the Spirit
is in control. We no longer gratify the deeds of the
flesh.

It is important to note how we end up in the situations we find ourselves in today. At some time, we per-
formed some act or series of actions that led us to this
point. We may have witnessed these actions in our
parents, friends, sisters, brothers, or college friends,

but these acts also began to surface in our own lives. We did them repeatedly, until they became *habits.*

After the acts become habits, the persistent repetition of these habits lead to the development of a *disposition*; we enter a position where we have to defend our actions and our habits. If anyone tries to change our habits or our acts, it causes us to have a bad disposition. Finally, we move into the last stage, where our will becomes involved. At this stage, we *choose* to do these acts and resulting habits that we know are wrong. When we have come this far, we cannot break free of these entanglements on our own because our wills have become involved.

When we become born again, we become filled with the Spirit. These deeds of the flesh, these acts, and these habits that lead to a bad disposition must be removed from our lives. We need to decide by the Spirit—by the power of the Spirit that rules over everything that is wrong in our lives, over wrong desires, wrong sinful actions, and dictates of the flesh—to halt this downward movement. We need to say, "No, I will decide by my heart. I will decide by my spirit. I will decide that I am no longer going to do these things. I am going to walk in the Spirit."

Once we have made this choice, the Spirit will begin to help us erase all the issues and areas of our lives that have developed through wrong acts, led to habits, and formed a disposition that affected our will and hindered our relationship with God. Our bad dispositions can be changed by the Holy Spirit.

Unholy desires are a product of our will. We tend to pursue those things that gratify the flesh. When we live according to the Spirit, we do not want to grieve the Holy Spirit. We do not want to hurt the Holy Spirit in any way. We do not want to spurn, quench, suppress, or subdue the Holy Spirit. Our desire is for the Holy Spirit to be alive in us, but this requires us to resist these acts and deeds of the flesh.

## Rivers of Living Water

*He who believes in Me [who cleaves to and trusts in and relies on Me] as the Scripture has said. From his innermost being shall flow [continuously] springs and rivers of living water* (John 7:38 AMP).

What comes out of the mind is law and rules. The mind is a dirty pool, but what comes out of the Spirit is life. Out of the belly flows rivers of living water, which is the Spirit.

When we believe in Him, the rivers of living water shall flow from us. Jesus said this concerning the Spirit that those who believed in Him would receive. Jesus said this when the Spirit was not yet given because Jesus was not yet glorified. But, hallelujah and glory, Jesus has been glorified since this experience that Jesus had with His disciples. We now have the glorified Christ. As a result, the Spirit in us is now the power that overcomes the law and helps us to put down the old law and bring in the Spirit of life.

When we believe in Jesus Christ, *we receive the Spirit, the same Spirit that raised Christ from the dead.* The cross is very important, and we do not diminish the work of the cross. However, without the resurrection and the glory that came through the resurrection, the power of the cross would be nullified. Many people died on crosses, but nobody except Jesus rose from the dead after crucifixion by the glory of God, walked again, spoke to people, and ascended to be seated at the right hand of God Almighty.

The same Spirit that raised Christ from the dead now dwells in us, and it can restore life to our mortal, short-lived, perishable bodies. If we have a physical abnormality or a physical infirmity of any kind and if we believe in Jesus Christ and the Spirit of God lives in us, we can have our mortal, short-lived, perishable body restored through the Spirit. We simply need to ask the Holy Spirit of God to fill us and restore that mortal, short-lived, perishable body to youthfulness and health.

By the power of the Holy Spirit, we can habitually change our temperament, our disposition, and our habits. Our acts and our physical body can change as a result of the indwelling Holy Spirit. In Christ, we share in His inheritance as a child, as an heir, and as a fellow heir with Christ. Because we share in His glory and in the Holy Spirit, we have help to change.

### Testimony

Spiritually, there was a time in my life when things were not going well for me, and yet God was still speaking to me and working in me. There were times I felt that I could not pray because my heart was not right. There was unforgiveness in my heart, and there were other areas that were wrong in my life. I came to God and confessed, "I just do not know what I am going to do. I cannot get hold of this situation." He spoke to my heart and said, "All I want you to do is just keep walking toward Me. Do not ever turn and go the other way. Just keep on walking toward Me. Believe that as you walk toward Me, those things will fall off your life and you will have victory."

Although I was still struggling in these areas, I obeyed His instructions to me. I continued to walk toward Him, and I continued to pray, believing He cared for me enough that He would hear my prayers. The time came when all the negative issues that I had been struggling with fell away, just as He told me they would.

## Crucified With Christ

When we submit ourselves to be crucified, when we die to self, dying to old habits, old acts, old dispositions, and areas of our lives that we wanted to control, then we cease to live in our own strength. We begin to rely on, adhere to, and have complete trust in the Son of God who brought us to the place of total deliverance.

We need to be lawbreakers because there is no way that we can come to God through the law. The only way to come to God is through Jesus Christ and through the Spirit.

Paul died to the law and the demands of the law so that he could live for God. Christ came to fulfill the law, and He did that through the crucifixion. We fulfilled the law by allowing our old man to be crucified. We must also allow the new man to come forth in the spirit and in power.

Christ came and He died; He did this work for us. Now we have the right to receive the ability and the power of the Spirit to grow in the things of the Spirit. We do not come to God through any actions of our own or through any rituals or words or plans or laws. There is nothing that can bring us to the Lord Jesus Christ, except the blood of Jesus, the cross, the resurrection, the ascension, the circumcision, the Holy Spirit cleansing, and the very grace of God.

## Perfected by Love

It is the love of God that constrains us and draws us to Himself. He gave us a new commandment and that was to love God with all our heart, soul, and mind, and our neighbors as ourselves (see Mk. 12:30-31). There is one law. There is one rule, and that is love. Paul talks about love many times. We have to be obedient to the heavenly vision. We have to do what God has called us to do and do it out of love. It is love that motivates us to be obedient.

We must become like Jesus because it is in Him that we live and move and have our being. It is through Christ that everything about us is perfected. We can never be perfected in the law, but we can be perfected in the Spirit. We can be perfected in Him.

We confess Jesus. We confess Jesus and not our failure. We confess Jesus and not the law. We confess Jesus and not emptiness. We confess Him as the Holy Spirit begins to bear us up and show us that we can be redeemed from the curse of the law, that all things can be brought together for our good, and that all comes through the Holy Spirit.

> *And He that searcheth the hearts knoweth what is the mind of the Spirit, because He maketh intercession for the saints according to the will of God. And we know that all things work together for good to them that love God, to them who are the called according to His purpose. For whom He did foreknow, He also did predestinate to be conformed to the image of His Son, that He might be the firstborn among many brethren* (Romans 8:27-29).

We can choose to do many good works in our lives, but if they are not the calling of God and not the will of God, the good works will come to naught. When we walk in the Spirit, we will know what God wants. We will live by the Spirit, and the Spirit will bear us up and carry us forward on the right path.

The Holy Spirit leads us and guides us until we come to the knowledge that He can raise us up while we are in this life. This position is one that we can never arrive at by following the law, but only by following the Holy Spirit.

### Personal Decision

I would ask you to search your own heart and decide, "Do I have this Holy Spirit, this powerful, powerful

Holy Spirit who can help me to change from the inside out? Do I have this Holy Spirit to guide me and put me on the right path that I might line my life up with the will of God according to His power?"

I believe the Holy Spirit power will become so valuable to you that you will see that you need to get away from the laws, rules, and plans of action that you have always put upon yourself and allow the Holy Spirit to guide and direct your life. His intent and His plan would be for you to do exactly what God would want for your life.

> *"Father, we thank You for this time that we have had together to consider Your ways. Lord, we pray that You will help us to see from this day forward that we need to come to You completely and in total reverence. We want to be reverent before You, coming to You, knowing that Your Holy Spirit power is going to bless us. We thank You for the Holy Spirit working in us, guiding us, directing us, bringing us to the perfect place where we will line up with the Spirit of God. We thank You. In Jesus' name, amen."*

# Chapter 6

# *Who We Are in Him*

Christ and the Church form the greatest mystery, which was once hidden and then was revealed to Paul in the Epistles. It is the message of being in Him—*Christ in you, the hope of glory*. When we become confident of the work of the Lord Jesus Christ, we will grow progressively closer to Him. This will draw us to the Holy Spirit, who is sent to guide us; to the angels, who are sent to accompany us; and to God Himself, who designed the whole plan.

> *For I am jealous over you with godly jealousy: for I have espoused you to one husband, that I may present you as a chaste virgin to Christ* (2 Corinthians 11:2).

Christ wants to come back for a pure, clean Bride. It is up to us to be obedient and to allow Him to cleanse us and make us perfect so that we might be perfect for Christ.

> *...If that which ye have heard from the beginning shall remain in you, ye also shall continue in the Son, and in the Father* (1 John 2:24)

### Eternal Life

This is the promise that He promised us, even eternal life. Christ in you, the hope of glory, is eternal life. Eternal Life is a person, not just a place. Eternity is a place where you will be, but Eternal Life in Him is a person.

> *And this is the record, that God hath given to us eternal life, and this life is in His Son. He that hath the Son hath life; and he that hath not the Son of God hath not life. These things have I written unto you that believe on the name of the Son of God; that ye may know that ye have eternal life, and that ye may believe on the name of the Son of God. And this is the confidence that we have in Him, that, if we ask any thing according to His will, He heareth us: and if we know that He hear us, whatsoever we ask, we know that we have the petitions that we desired of Him. If any man see his brother sin a sin which is not unto death, he shall ask, and he shall give him life for them that sin not unto death. There is a sin unto death: I do not say that he shall pray for it. All unrighteousness is sin: and there is a sin not unto death. We know that whosoever is born of God sinneth not; but he that is begotten of God keepeth himself, and that wicked one toucheth him not. And we know that we*

*are of God, and the whole world lieth in wickedness. And we know that the Son of God is come, and hath given us an understanding, that we may know Him that is true, and we are in Him that is true, even in His Son Jesus Christ. This is the true God, and eternal life* (1 John 5:11-20).

Eternal Life is a person, Jesus Christ. When we go to be in Him in Heaven, we will be in God. All His creation will become one at that time. Yet God is seeking that now, in us while we are here on this earth. He wants us to become so close to Him and have such a wonderful relationship with Him that, when we receive Him, we become sons of God. In Him we come together into one. We become part of the whole Body of Christ.

We have not received a spirit of bondage or fear, which separates, but we have received adoption and become part of the Body and the family of God. Knowing that God abides within us gives us total joy and freedom. He will be a Father to us, if we will simply choose to be His child. He has redeemed us that we might receive adoption. From the beginning, His plan has been for us to be accepted into the family.

### Divine Protection

*And the Lord said unto him, Go through the midst of the city, through the midst of Jerusalem, and set a mark upon the foreheads of the men that sigh and that cry for all the abominations that be done in the midst thereof* (Ezekiel 9:4).

Ezekiel is saying that those who are marked with the mark will not be touched with destruction. He told the angel to go through the streets of Jerusalem and put a mark on the forehead of the intercessors. This was to seal them so that they would be kept, protected from any danger. God has also sealed us. He has put a mark on us—the blood of Jesus Christ. When we recognize that we are set apart, we will have reverential fear of God. In Ezekiel, the mark was put on those who were angry at sin, angry at their own sin, or who were humble before God. These people were crying, "God, help me. I am a sinner. God, help me. I am a failure. Help me. I need Your help." Those are the ones whom God wanted to help. Those who said that they did not need His help were the ones who had to die.

*If we suffer, we shall also reign with Him: if we deny Him, He also will deny us: if we believe not, yet He abideth faithful: He cannot deny Himself* (2 Timothy 2:12-13).

God requires our obedience and faithfulness. We must love Him with such depth that there is no desire to deny Him. If we deny Him, He must deny us. But, if we remain faithful to Him, even if we pull away slightly, He cannot deny us because He will not deny Himself. He has placed the Christ in us, whom He cannot deny.

*Who hath also sealed us, and given the earnest of the Spirit in our hearts* (2 Corinthians 1:22).

He marked us with a mark that would separate us and keep us from the death angel. He also sealed us with the Holy Spirit. He wooed us with the Holy Spirit, creating an earnestness in our hearts to come to Christ.

## We Are Marked

As our understanding of God increases, we recognize Him, His Son, the Holy Spirit, and other Christians more readily. We can walk into a room full of people, into an airport, a crowded bus, a train, or plane, and pick out other Christians because we will sense that there is something special about them. They are sealed. They have His name written on them. Nobody sees the name, yet the Spirit of Christ will be evident.

## Testimony

On one occasion, I had to pick up three ladies in a large airport because they were coming to visit the Bible Study Fellowship that I was attending. I did not know who they were, and the ladies did not know each other. I was told that I would not have any trouble picking them out—I would know them. As the passengers came off the plane, I immediately noticed my passengers and approached them. I asked if they were the ones I was to take to the lodge for the conference. They each said, "Yes," and then asked me how I knew them. I told them that it had been easy; I looked at their faces. I could tell which were the Christians when they came off the plane.

We have been sealed with His name, and it is apparent to others. That is why it is so important to walk in newness of life, in righteousness, and in humility. We must walk in such a way that God can bless us and bless others through us. That is when we are being fruitful in every good work.

## Knit Together

We are part of the Body of Christ, a body designed for love to flow between all its members. Not only should love be displayed among us, but we should all have a place to serve God in the Body. We should each serve Him in our position, fulfilling our purpose. When we are fellowshipping within the Body, we draw strength from one another. There is purpose for the Body of Christ to function together. We cannot grow until we see that we have been put together to function as a unit.

*And not holding the Head, from which all the body by joints and bands having nourishment ministered, and knit together, increaseth with the increase of God* (Colossians 2:19).

Knit together means we are glued together, connected, interconnected, knitted together in our hearts. The body is an organism, which consists of numerous cells. Each cell works in conjunction with the others, and all need each other. It is important for us to fellowship with other Christians. We can glean from them, and they can glean from us. We need to make ourselves available to various groups within the Body of Christ so that we may draw strength from one another.

First Corinthians 12 explains that the spiritual gifts are given for one purpose, which is for the unity of the believers, to make us members of Christ's Body. That is the reason for the different types of gifts. Each one has a different gift, something unique to share with the rest of the Body. All the gifts given to the Body and for the Body are listed in Ephesians 4, Romans 12, and First Corinthians 12. The Body cannot be the Body without all the parts functioning in their proper position. We cannot have all feet or all hands or all arms or all eyes. Everybody has to have a different part, and every part has to supply the other parts.

## The Best Gift

First Corinthians 12:27-31 says that we should covet the best gifts. Which of these gifts is the best gift? It is the one needed at the time. To meet the needs that we encounter, it may take a different selection of gifts each time. One time the necessary gift may be prophecy. Another time, encouragement may be needed. Still another occasion may require tongues, interpretation, healing, or whatever the Holy Spirit determines.

When we are in tune with God, we will be a source of blessing and power. Everything has been put under Christ's feet, and when we are in Him, all things are under our feet. This includes satan, sickness, fear, and everything negative that tries to stop the move of God.

## Leadership Serves

Leadership is sent to the Body of Christ to serve. God sends leaders to train the members to do the work of the ministry. Everyone needs to serve one another, and as we do, God will bless us. Whenever we faithfully and humbly serve the Lord, blessings will always come back to us. When we are humble before God, a humility that is of Him, then He will promote us. That is a promise. He raises us up when we humble ourselves.

## Kingdom of God

*Blessed are the poor in spirit: for theirs is the kingdom of heaven* (Matthew 5:3).

Daniel foresaw a Kingdom of God where all would come together and offer a relationship that would be within the reach of all persons. The Old Testament prophets were given these messages time after time, but Paul was called to bring them all together. This revelation, this mystery, which Paul speaks of repeatedly, was given to him because he was humble enough to keep the vision, the mystery, the revelation that was given to him and pour it out for the Body. Jesus Christ gave him the mystery of the Church, the Body of Christ, and the Kingdom of God. He entrusted him with these incredible revelations.

## Pleasing God

When we please God, men will be pleased with us also. I learned at the very beginning of my walk with the Lord that if a man and wife (or two friends, two co-workers, or two people in any other type of relationship) spent all their time looking to God and pleasing God in everything they did, they would automatically please one another. If each person was pleasing God 100 percent, they would please each other. If either one was not pleasing God 100 percent, there would be contention, arguments, disharmony, misunderstandings, miscommunications, and anger. But, if we are truly pleasing God 100 percent in our hearts and each person is pleasing God 100 percent, there will be a perfect relationship. Our purpose is to please God first, before anything else.

## A Peculiar People

God wants a people, a special people for Himself. In Deuteronomy, He talked about us being a peculiar people unto Himself (see Deut. 14:2). He said that He had not called the Israelites because they were the biggest; in fact, they were the smallest (see Deut. 7:6-7). He called them because He wanted a people to call upon His name and to be close to Him. God is still looking for a people, a group of people who will love one another and call God, Father. He wants a people who are willing to say, "Abba, Abba, Father, Father," a people who are willing to lean on one another in the Body of Christ as children of God. He desires a group willing to be sealed with the promise, to receive all the blessings as adopted sons, to be obedient children, and to be humble before God. When we do all these things, we will become what God has been looking for: the Israel of this day.

He wants to make us a Church, a Bride that is perfect, ready, willing, and capable of receiving the King to come, our Bridegroom. The time is coming, but we are not quite ready yet, or He would be here. If each one of us did our job to get ourselves ready, I believe that He would come soon. Let us pray and believe God that we would recognize our place in the Body. Every one of us has a unique position, and we need to know our place and fill it.

> *"Father God, I ask You to reveal to us our position in the Body of Christ by the blessed Holy Spirit, the one who brings us the message, helps us to understand it, and then guides us when we do not know how to pray. As the Bible says, the Holy Spirit prays the perfect will of God for us. Father, we release ourselves to You, and we say, 'God touch us, guide us, and direct us.' Help us in this walk toward You that we might know who we are and that we might be obedient sons and daughters. Help us to call upon the Lord Jesus Christ, allowing ourselves to be marked, even to be sealed, according to Your purposes, that You would bring those blessings to us. God, we thank You for this word. We count it an honor to come before You in this way. In Jesus' name, amen."*

# Chapter 7

# *What We Have in Him*

In the last chapter we shared about who we are in Him in our adoption as sons of God. We are sealed by the Holy Spirit. We are the sons of God. We are brought into the beloved, made part of the full Kingdom of God and of the family of God, and are brought together in Him. It is through Him and in Him that we have all that we have. There is nothing we have that is not given to us by Jesus Christ, who is the power of God in our lives.

When we are in Him, what do we have? What we have inside us gives us a relationship, an interrelationship with God, with Jesus, and with the Holy Spirit that enables us to become more like Jesus Christ.

Our position in Him gives us access to all the abilities resident in the fullness of God. We have the attributes of God, and His character becomes available to us when we are in Him. We will begin to hear God speak and hear revelation knowledge. We will begin to hear the mysteries unfolding, receive truth and instruction within our hearts, and hear His still, small voice. Then, we will be empowered to go, do, and be all that He has called us to be. The fullness of the Godhead working in us will express itself in our lives.

### God Is...

When we think about the characteristics of God and who He is, our thoughts turn to faith, love, power, creative ability, light, life, glory, grace, peace, spirit, and many other attributes. With Him in us and us in Him, we also exhibit these characteristics. Expressing the character of God that is inside us releases the ability of God to make wonder-working power available now. How can we arrive at the full potential of the ability of God that is available to us?

### Hearing

One of the first areas that we have to develop to reach our full potential of the ability of God is our hearing. When God is in us, the power of God is also resident within us. The temple is no longer in Jerusalem; it is within our spirits. It has become part of us, and God has a place to transfer information. He has a place to deposit life. He has a place to deposit truth, so it can come back out again. How does it come back out? We have to learn how to listen. We have to know how to receive and bring forth this revelation knowledge, these mysteries that have been held for centuries. God wants them made known and given to the Body of Christ in the right season.

## Parable of the Sower

Jesus spoke to the multitudes and He gave them the message of the parable of the sower. The disciples took Him aside and inquired of Him, "Why is it that you talk that way when you are with the people, but when you are with us, you talk another way?" He said, "You are the ones who are supposed to hear. If they had ears to hear they would hear, but they do not have ears to hear." He commended them for their hearing ear. (See Matthew 13.) We must cultivate our hearing ear by heeding the still, small voice.

## The Shepherd's Voice

In Israel, shepherds take their sheep down from their hills to a shared watering hole. The shepherds gather together to talk, and all their sheep mingle and they mix. To a casual observer, it appears the sheep are confused, not knowing whose they are, as they mix and share the water together. But when the shepherd prepares to leave, he makes a unique noise with bells or musical instruments, speaks a phrase, or sings, and every one of his sheep will separate from the larger group and follow him. Likewise, every other shepherd, whether there were four or five or ten shepherds, when he leaves, the sheep that are in his fold know his voice and leave with him. When he leaves, they disassemble themselves and go with their leader because they know his voice. That is the way we are with our

Shepherd. In our inner man, we can hear the still, small voice of the Holy Spirit, the Spirit of Christ, the voice of God inside us. We know to follow that voice and will not follow any other voice.

> *To him the porter openeth; and the sheep hear his voice: and he calleth his own sheep by name, and leadeth them out* (John 10:3).

Jesus Christ is the shepherd of our soul and of our heart today. There is one flock, and Christ is our Shepherd. He is the Shepherd. He is the one who speaks to us, and His is the voice we heed. God speaks to us in many ways, but the most prevalent way He speaks is by the still, small voice in our inner man.

### The Channel

We are branches. Jesus is the vine, and God is the root. Inside every tree, there are channels for the sap to run from the root, to the branch, and ultimately, to the leaves and to the fruit. These channels within the branches, within each "member" of a tree or a vine, are there to make way for the life-giving properties of the root to come into the fruit. We have the Holy Spirit who accomplishes this in us. We are branches of the Vine. We will be fed, and we will hear. These messages will go back and forth, similar to a telephone line. The messages will come as the Holy Spirit speaks. He instructs us and brings the word from the Father. John 14 states that the Comforter will teach us all things. He will bring to our remembrance what it is that we need.

## The Still, Small Voice

Other ways for the Holy Spirit to speak is through other men and women of God, through messages of God. For me, personally, the words with the most impact are those that I hear from the still, small voice within me. I can hear a wonderful message that may move my soul and heart and make a difference in my life, but when I hear the still, small voice, I know that it is my Master speaking to me. He may be saying that there is someone in the room who needs healing in a specific area or that there is a person hurting within their emotions. Whatever He says to me is a message that I cherish. The still, small voice from the Holy Spirit, especially as He speaks at my first moment of consciousness in the morning, makes the strongest impression on me. I can always follow that voice.

We can enjoy the tremendous teachings of men and women of God. Their teachings may be good messages, and they may present truth, light, peace, and joy. However, the bottom line is that each of us must go directly to the Lord and receive from Him through His still, small voice, His truth for our lives. God also speaks to us through angels. He still does that today. I do not believe that He did that just for Mary and Joseph and Zachariah. I do not believe that use of divine messengers was just for the days of old. I believe that angels still bring us messages from the Father.

## His Presence

When God reveals His presence, we may experience a stirring in our souls. Seated in heavenly places with Christ, we will not hear the voice of the enemy. There is no way that we can be seated in heavenly places, listening to the voice of God and experiencing His presence, and listen to the voice of the enemy at the same time. When we are seated in heavenly places in Him, be assured that the devil has no place to speak to our minds or hearts. If he speaks to us, we must have separated ourselves from the throne room. There is no sin consciousness in the throne room; no devil or unbelief can be carried into the throne room. We need to ask the Lord to enable us to be in the throne room with Him so that we might hear His voice and hear Him perfectly.

There are many people who want to hear, but they do not have a hearing ear because they have not allowed themselves to believe that God wants to speak to them individually. It is not a great mystery. It is not a "far-out" experience. It is merely God within us, speaking sweet, gentle mysteries to our hearts.

## Mystery

What is a *mystery*? A mystery is something that we believe by faith. It is something that we accept by faith and truly believe can come to pass. One of the mysteries is Christ incarnate. He came from God, of course, and He came through Mary, by a virgin birth. It is very difficult to believe that someone can be born of a virgin birth, but in our hearts this mystery is revealed.

It requires faith to serve a God that we cannot see, to accept the death of a man that we had not personally met, and to receive glory from a resurrection from the dead that we did not witness. We live by principles set down in the hearts of men whom we do not know. We experience power from a source that we are not able to see—except by pure faith. These are all mysteries. These are all revealed truths, revelation. These are truths that we accept, which *Christ, the hope of glory*, reveals to us.

## Salvation and Healing

A few of the other mysteries that we experience are salvation and healing. How do these things happen? We cannot explain them, but what we do know is that they are realities that we believe by faith. The Word of God says that salvation and healing are possible. Because we believe that the Word is true and truth, the mystery happens. We are healed, saved, and receive other promises available in the Word.

## The Hope Within

Mysteries presented in Colossians are the mysteries of the Kingdom of God, of light and life—*Christ in you, the hope of glory*, and being seated in heavenly places. Our hope is within; from the foundation of the world, this hope has been planted in us. We are winners, having received all that has been promised. Our participation is believing that God is bringing forth our answers and victories. We have our needs met in Him, and by faith we see the answers come forth.

## Glory

*If ye then be risen with Christ, seek those things which are above, where Christ sitteth on the right hand of God* (Colossians 3:1).

The glory of God, which is His presence, is designed to be our dwelling place. The glory cloud, the glory experience of being in the Body of Christ, and the glory of being raised to sit with Him in heavenly places, are all awesome experiences that we should seek.

A mystery is anything that is beyond human understanding. A mystery cannot be comprehended by the human mind. This information was revealed to Paul, and that is why Paul received so many afflictions and sufferings. He had tremendous truth and knowledge of God and was constantly bombarded by the enemy. Yet Paul maintained his joy; he kept his life on the path in pursuit of the call of God on his life. He was not deterred from fulfilling his call, which was revealing the mysteries God had entrusted to him.

### Face to Face

Understanding a mystery is only possible by the power of God, and it must be accepted by faith. Through the experiential knowledge of God and a personal commitment to God, we must develop a relationship with Him to the level of Moses, who knew God face to face. At that point, we will experience His relationship, not only from within, but even from without, just as Jesus did throughout the Old Testament and the New Testament. Jesus was present throughout the Old Testament, but once He took on an earthly body through Mary, His sole commitment was to be the Christ, the Son of the living God.

Moses saw God face to face in the Old Testament. He saw the power of God. The glory that came upon Moses caused him to cover his face with a veil so that others could look upon him. No flesh could look upon that glory. It was too powerful and overwhelming.

Moses wrote a lot of the Old Testament. Paul, like Moses, met Jesus face to face. He, subsequently, wrote two-thirds of the New Testament. He met with Him in the deserts of Arabia. Jesus came to Paul in personal revelation, showing him who He was and what He was. It was a transforming experience. Many of us have those transforming experiences, but we are afraid of them. Sometimes we may not even recognize these God happenings. Let us not miss our day of visitation.

*At midday, O king, I saw in the way a light from heaven, above the brightness of the sun, shining round about me and them which journeyed with me* (Acts 26:13).

In this passage, Paul is explaining to the king what he experienced while traveling to carry out his mission to persecute Christians. In his encounter, Jesus Christ came to Paul personally and said that He was going to show him things that he would not believe even if he saw them. He told Paul that he was going to believe them because they would have a communication that was powerful. We have that communication available to us today. It is ours. There is no reason that we cannot have a Paul experience and have the power of God come upon us. The comprehension of the power that is inside us will change us. With this experience, we will never go back to being the old man that we used to be. We are marked by these powerful encounters with God and are never the same.

Many of us have had these experiences, but we may have put them aside feeling that maybe they were too extreme. But let us consider Paul's encounter: Jesus Christ appeared to him personally, spoke to him, and told him not to fight "against the pricks" (see Acts 26:14). Paul was about to die to self and everything that he had been taught and believed. He had been resisting the prodding of Jesus, even persecuting with a vengeance those who believed in Him.

Jesus will come as He came to Paul. He will appear for a purpose, which is to make us ministers and witnesses of both the things that we see and those things in which He will appear. Jesus will give us a deeper, fuller revelation and spiritual light than unbelievers can comprehend. He will provide enlightenment that will lead us through spiritual experiences of which we will testify forever.

### God Revealed

At times when the spirit of revelation has been poured into us and we receive powerful revelations from God, we get so excited that we want to share these revelations with everybody. But as we mature, we understand that sometimes we can share these insights, and sometimes we must keep them to ourselves. There are times that we hear for ourselves, personally, and what we hear is not necessarily for the whole Body of Christ. The Spirit of God speaks to our inner man and gives us revelation knowledge. The Spirit reveals insights that we may not be able to discuss.

> *Jesus saith unto him, Have I been so long time with you, and yet hast thou not known Me, Philip? he that hath seen Me hath seen the Father; and how sayest thou then, Shew us the Father? Believest thou not that I am in the Father, and the Father in Me? the words that I speak unto you I speak not of Myself: but the Father that dwelleth in Me, He doeth the works. Believe Me that I am in the Father, and the Father in Me: or else believe Me for the very works' sake* (John 14:9-11).

God was in Jesus and revealed and manifested Himself to Him. Jesus said that if we have seen Him, we have seen God. If we have seen God, we have seen Jesus. There are times when we want to do the works of Jesus and we are not sure how we should pray. Jesus and the Father are so closely linked that if we say in the name of Jesus, the Father hears. If we say, "God, help me," Jesus is ready. Either way, we need to pray to the Father in the name of Jesus, and God will hear us because the Father and Son are one. There is a love relationship between the two, and They have sent us the indwelling Holy Spirit. The Spirit will help, guide, and manifest revelations of the heart of God to us as He did to Jesus.

If we love Jesus, He promised that we would know Him and that He would come and abide in us (see Jn. 14:23; 1 Jn. 4:7-8). We are called to love God and the Body of Christ. If we really love God, whom we cannot see, we must love the brethren whom we can see (see 1 Jn. 4:20). There are aspects in our lives that we must allow the Spirit of God to cleanse and change because God is anxious and ready for a people to be like Him. He wants to indwell and empower His people with might. He longs for a purified Bride who is ready for her Bridegroom. Until we become the spotless Bride that He has planned for us to be, He cannot come again and bring the full revelation of Jesus Christ to the earth. However, when He does come, we will experience complete and total peace, love, and deliverance from the enemy. It is our responsibility to prepare ourselves as the Bride and to allow the spirit of revelation to flourish in our hearts and lives and to bring life to others.

*"Father, we thank You for the mystery, for the spiritual revelation, for the understanding of who we are in Christ. God, we want to thank You for the blessing that will come from this knowledge that we have and from this understanding and from the wisdom that comes from Your being in us. We thank You, Father, and we count it an honor to hold that glory within us. God, we want to understand more and more and more how we can live the ascended life, how we can come directly to You and deal directly with You. We thank You, Father, for this blessing. We want to bless You. In Jesus' name, amen!"*

# Chapter 8

# *Victory and Anointing in His Name*

Victory and anointing are found in the name of Jesus. His name holds the foundation of all that He is and all that He can and will provide. The most radical, life-changing gift we receive when we believe in the name of Jesus is salvation. Romans 10:9 says that if we believe on Jesus' name, we will be saved; it is a matter of believing in the character and name of Jesus. God sent forth His Son that we might believe on His name.

> *But as many as received Him, to them gave He power to become the sons of God, even to them that believe on His name* (John 1:12).

There is purpose and position in a person's name; the name is the character of the person. For instance, someone who worked with coal once became called

*Coalman*; a man who was a cook or baker was called *Baker*, and one who fished for a living became *Fisher*. Many family names signify what they have done in the past and their type of business. A name can often be wrapped up in character, such as, Peter the Rock, Simon the Stone, Jesus the Savior, and Christ the Messiah. When we say His name, we are saying, "He is my Messiah. He is the one through whom God sent miracles and healing." When we say the name of Jesus Christ, we are saying we believe in Jesus, in His saving ability, in Christ, the Messiah, the Anointed One, the one who was sent.

In Exodus 3 Moses asked God what he should say to the children of Israel.

*And God said unto Moses, I AM THAT I AM: and He said, Thus shalt thou say unto the children of Israel, I AM hath sent me unto you* (Exodus 3:14).

The George M. Lamsa translation of Exodus 3:14 renders it in a different way completely, and it is very expressive:

*And God said to Moses, I am AHIAH ASHAR HIGH (that is, THE LIVING GOD); and He said, Thus you shall say to the children of Israel: AHIAH has sent me to you.*

When Moses told the children of Israel, "God said to me, 'I AM,' " he was saying that the living God had sent him to them.

When we believe in the living God, we believe God can supply any need and accomplish any task. Praying in the name of Jesus invokes His personal response, and He will do it. He will grant what we ask in His name. If we ask in His name, He goes to work to see that the thing is done. Whatever we ask in His name, presenting all that He is, will be granted because He wants the Father to be glorified. Jesus and the Holy Spirit want the Father glorified.

> *And I will do [I Myself will grant] whatever you shall ask in My Name [as presenting all that I AM], so that the Father may be glorified and extolled in (through) the Son* (John 14:13 AMP).

When we pray in the Spirit, we are praying the will of God. When we pray in the name of Jesus, we are asking Jesus to bring forth the answers to our requests. There is no more effective form of prayer than praying the will of God.

If we had known as teenagers that our father or mother would have said yes when we asked for the car, we would not have had butterflies and frustration when we asked for the car. We would have said something like, "I know that you are going to say yes, so is it okay if I take the car now?" But, if we had known there would be a problem, we may have stuttered and been apprehensive when we made our request because we were afraid the answer would be no.

Knowing the will of God in a given situation allows us to approach it with gladness, peace, and joy because we know we are assured of our answer. We can be confident because we are asking the will of God and asking in the name of Jesus. *This is praying about what we are going to pray before we pray.* We pray and ask God what He would have us pray. We ask the Holy Spirit to guide us in the will of the Lord for the circumstances. This helps us to get our answers very quickly. By praying the Word and the will of God, we will experience tremendous success in our prayer life.

Prayers uttered through selfish motives, instead of the will of God, are seldom answered. The Holy Spirit wants God to get the glory, but when we pray by carnal desires, God gets no glory. When we are first born again, the Lord may answer requests we present because He wants to establish a relationship. Later, when we mature, He withholds answers to selfish requests. He wants us to mature in our prayer life and in our relationship with Him. If we pray in the Holy Spirit, by the Holy Spirit, and pray the will and Word of God, we will receive a positive response. Any self or selfish motivations in prayer may cause the answer to be negative. If we pray in the name of Jesus in the will of God, we will receive healing, miracles, or whatever we need.

The living God, the *Ahaya*, the I AM, testified of the Son of God, saying, "This is My beloved Son...hear ye Him" (Mt. 17:5b). The disciples also came and testified of Jesus. They wrote the books of their testimony because of Jesus Christ, the Messiah, who came and worked the works in their midst. We believe in the Messiah, the Christ, the Son of the living God, Christ in you, the hope of glory, and we experience the fulfillment of His plan.

## Testimony

We are commanded to use the name of Jesus; this is how we get the Father's attention.

When I was a young child, there was a little grocery store where my father had a charge account. I could go there, pick up a loaf of bread, approach the owner, and tell him to put the price of the bread on my father's bill. Using my father's name allowed me to walk out with a loaf of bread. As I left, I would be at total peace, for I had received approval from my father and agreement of the owner of the store that I could take the bread. My mission was accomplished successfully because I presented the name and will of my father.

Even this story is no comparison to our position with our heavenly Father, who owns the cattle on a thousand hills. He owns everything, from the cells in our bodies to the air that we breathe. He wants to supply our needs with His limitless resources. His name brings us health, peace, and a life worth living. When we ask Him in His name, He is excited to bless us. In obedience to His command, we should use the name of Jesus.

*Behold, what manner of love the Father hath bestowed upon us, that we should be called the sons of God: therefore the world knoweth us not, because it knew Him not. Beloved, now are we the sons of God, and it doth not yet appear what we shall be: but we know that, when He shall appear, we shall be like Him; for we shall see Him as He is* (1 John 3:1-2).

God wants us to be like His Son and to have the peace of God and the joy of the Lord working in us. As He is—full of peace and joy—we too should be in this world.

The Greek word for offspring is *genos*. It means genes, as in *generation* and as in *genes*—that character that goes from person to person or that is passed to one's *offspring*. We are the offspring of God. We have His fruit, abilities, and personality. We are part of the family of God, the begotten, like Christ who was the first begotten.

## Testimony

Miracle-working power is available when we use the name of Jesus.

I ministered to a woman recently who had polyps and ulcers down in her throat that were too far down to be reached with external treatments. I prayed for her in the name of Jesus and then went home. The following week she testified that all pain was gone the day after we prayed. She went back to the doctor for her checkup, and he told her that there was no reason to take any more medication because the ulcers were gone. The type of ulcer was one that, according to the doctor, should have lingered for months. She expected a long siege in this illness, but the name of Jesus transcended the laws of nature. The name of Jesus changed that part of her throat and wiped away all the ulcers and infection, and she was healed. The name of Jesus did the job. I did nothing but believe, and the power of God worked through the name of Jesus.

## Miracle-Working Power

To receive miracle-working power, we must first grasp the revelation of who God is, who Jesus is, who the Holy Spirit is, and what the significance of the Word is. When we have this revelation, we will no longer merely "parrot" words. Our words will have power and meaning. Revealed knowledge uncovers the power of God that enables us to receive from God instantly. Then we are able to call on the Father, with the name of Jesus, and use the power of the Spirit and the Word to see miracles come to pass. Miracle-working power is the Holy Spirit enabling us beyond our own ability.

The second requirement to receive miracle-working power is to understand the mystery of the ascended life. Revelation knowledge opens the door. We can begin to accept the miracle, the mystery, the understanding of *Christ in you, the hope of glory*, and the completed work of Jesus Christ.

Another of the requirements to receive miracle-working power is the revelation of how the Holy Spirit works with us. This spiritual truth revealed to our hearts gives us solidity, assurance, and direction that we know the ways of God and His plans for us. It is no longer a hit-and-miss situation; rather, we know that when we pray the will of God, He hears and answers our prayers.

After we receive the revelation of who God is, understand the mystery, and learn to work with the Holy Spirit, we proceed into the understanding of His fullness. When we receive the fullness of the Godhead and His fullness resides in us, we have all the knowledge, wisdom, redemption power, and abilities of God. Once we begin to recognize that grace and truth abide in us, virtue and excellence will carry us. These blessings of God move us onward with peace.

### The Glory Revealed

As we read the Scripture and ask God to pour into us peace and direction, we will experience glory. When the glory cloud is present, ability becomes available for miracle-working power. Many people experience and respond to the glory in different ways. The glory comes as we honor God. The glory is a way for God to reveal Himself on the earth. Because He is spirit, He manifests Himself in a spiritual manner. In experiencing the glory, some people see a light, some people feel the presence, others see a cloud, others say they hear angels, still others taste things. Psalm 34:8 states, "O taste and see that the Lord is good...." The glory manifests in some people as a burning sensation, and they feel tremendous heat. Others feel cold and have goosebumps. The glory comes in different ways to different people.

We know that when we see glory, the Lord is close. As Stephen was being stoned by the angry crowd, he saw the glory of God as the heavens were opened (see Acts 7). The glory is available to us, and we do not have to be martyred to be able to approach that glory. Yes, we will go through persecutions and sufferings, but we can still experience the glory of God.

## Anointing

The anointing is a spiritual force; it is God working through our spirits to minister to His children by and through the Holy Spirit. The anointing is God Himself flowing. It is the Spirit Himself flowing in floods of power. There are waves of God's anointing that cause the gifts to flow.

> *And, behold, I send the promise of My Father upon you: but tarry ye in the city of Jerusalem, until ye be endued with power from on high* (Luke 24:49).

God wants to clothe us with anointing. He wants to clothe us with spiritual power, with an outpouring of Himself through the name of Jesus. He wants us to have the anointing that we may be a benefit to His Body. Most of the time, the anointing is not for us personally; it is for the Body. He wants this anointing and ability to flow through us, thus drawing people to Himself.

Many have read about Smith Wigglesworth. Smith was so close to God that as he walked down the street—not even preaching, just walking down the street—people would be convicted, drop to their knees, and ask God to forgive them of their sins. Somehow they knew to do that because the presence of God was so strong on Smith.

The Holy Spirit came upon the apostles, and His power has been transferred down through the ages and is available today. The Holy Spirit came just as Jesus promised when He told the disciples to wait until they were endued with power from on high (see Lk. 24:49).

When the disciples asked Jesus about the future, which was what they thought was important, Jesus put them aside. The important thing to Jesus was that they be filled with the Spirit, consumed with the glory cloud. He wanted them to think about miracle-working power, the mystery, revelation knowledge, and all the things that the power of the Holy Spirit can do. The times and seasons were not their business; Jesus' return was between Him and the Father. Jesus' concern was that the disciples receive the power of the Holy Spirit and that they do the will of the Father.

When we are in Him, we have the ability to put aside all our questions about the rapture—what it is, when it may take place, how it will happen, how many will go, whether there will be signs, etc. These questions are not our business. Our business is to be filled with the Spirit, to be anointed by God, and to go about doing good as Jesus did.

God anointed us with the Holy Spirit and power. Now we can go about doing good and healing all who are oppressed of the devil, for God is with us. We can turn Acts 10:38 into a very personal Scripture. There is an anointing, there is an unction, and there is an ability for us when we are in Him and when we know what His name means. When we are in Him, we are then able to use His name.

When we go to foreign fields, we teach the power of the name of Jesus for healing, and they are healed.

There is no "Plan B"; there is only the name of Jesus. They arrive at the same place at which we should arrive every time we say the name of Jesus. It is a glorious, glorious name. Within it is healing and miracle-working power. Within it is purpose and the answers to our prayers, if we simply use the name of Jesus.

## Security

Being in Him is the most secure place that we will ever be in our lives. When we know who we are in Him, everything and anything can go on around us, and we will still be at peace. Our hearts will remain full of joy.

*"Father, we thank You that we can come to You in the powerful name of Jesus, the name that is above all names. The name at which everyone will have to bow. There is only one 'Name' and that is the name of Jesus. We thank You, Father, that in His name we put before You our needs. We come to You for physical needs and for financial needs. God, carry us into a new realm of understanding Your purpose in our lives, knowing that we will never be hungry if we seek first the kingdom of God and His righteousness. Thank You, Father, that You are blessing us already, as we know Your principles, know You, and have believed in Your name. We have received You and have accepted You. Now we receive Your healing power and Your delivering power from poverty. We thank You for the blessings of God, the peace of God, and the joy of God that will go forth in our lives as we use the name of Jesus. We believe that as we present His*

*name, we present the living God, the great I AM, the power of God in the Holy Spirit. Thank You, Father, for this new understanding. In Jesus' name, amen!"*

# Chapter 9

# *The Ascended Life in Him*

After we have progressed in righteousness through the "in Him" message, we know who we are. We will have received Jesus and the Holy Spirit and will be filled with Christ. We will know who Christ is and know who God is, and finally, we will know who we are. Once we know these things, we enter a new realm, the "*ascended life* in Him."

This message is probably one that satan hates most, for once we understand who God is, who we are, and whose we are, we can also understand who the enemy is and experience total victory over him. Once we are grafted into the vine, the ability of God can flow through us unhindered. We can be the way to Jesus Christ for our friends. We can be the truth for them. We can be the ones who give them truth and lead them to eternal life—Jesus Christ. We can stand in the gap on the earth for Him, representing all that He is.

## Servant

*If any man serve Me, let him follow Me; and where I am, there shall also My servant be: if any man serve Me, him will My Father honour* (John 12:26).

Wherever Jesus is, that is where His servants are. If we are servants, we can be with Jesus—right now. Where is Jesus, now? He is at the right hand of the Father. How do we get there? That is what this whole chapter is about; that is the ascended life. In the above passage, Jesus was effectively saying, "If any man serve Me, let him follow Me wherever I go—into the throne room, into the Holy Place, into Heaven itself. Where I am, there shall My servant be. If any man serve Me, him will My Father honor and say come."

We are children of God. He instructs us to follow Him. His servants may follow Him wherever He is. We are His servants. Jesus said that we know the way and that we will know the way. It may not be visibly evident how we will do this, but Jesus works in the invisible. He works by the Spirit, and only the Holy Spirit can take us where He is.

## Risen With Him

*If ye then be risen with Christ, seek those things which are above, where Christ sitteth on the right hand of God* (Colossians 3:1).

This is not a position that we will attain in the "sweet by and by." This is an ascended life in the wonderful *here and now*. We long for the Kingdom of God to come upon the earth. All creation groans and travails for a deeper relationship with the Lord Jesus Christ (see Rom. 8:22-23).

In the Gospels of Matthew, Mark, and Luke are accounts of Jesus' transfiguration. He allowed three disciples to witness this heavenly encounter. Because this was before they had experienced the power of the Holy Spirit, they were awestruck and wanted to build three· tabernacles. They wanted to stop at this experience and memorialize it. However, God did not want them to be content with being on the outside looking in. He wanted them to continue in their walk and to go on into the ascended life. He allowed them to have this experience, not to be filled and puffed up because they saw Jesus in the glory, but because God wanted them to walk in the glory and lead others into this life. He wanted the disciples filled with power so that they could go and save multitudes.

God wants us to see Him; He wants us to see His glory. Jesus was the first fruit in all things. He had to experience transfiguration before anyone else could see or experience it. Our hope then is not in the rapture; but our hope is in Christ. Our hope is not in today's life. It is in faith, the God-kind of faith. By this faith of the Son of God, we ascend into the heavenlies.

*Which He wrought in Christ, when He raised Him from the dead, and set Him at His own right hand in the heavenly places* (Ephesians 1:20).

Christ is in the heavenlies now. We are connected to Him spiritually. We are in the world, but we are not of this world (see Jn. 17:16). We do not set our affections on earthly things any longer, but we set our affections on heavenly things. In the prayer that Jesus gave the disciples, He prayed, "...in earth, as it is in heaven" (Mt. 6:10), and we can pray this way also. But first, we must know the Christ, the Son of the living God. This is the key to the Kingdom of Heaven.

It is by our spirit that we are connected to Him. Our spirit man—that part of us that consists of intuition, conscience, and communion—becomes greatly heightened when we are in the presence of God. We must choose to be lifted up from the earthly feelings and experiences and to be raised and ascended above them into Heaven with Him. We are ascended with Him. We live on this earth, but we are ascended in the spirit man in heavenly places.

When we come to know the Lord Jesus Christ, who is seated in heavenly places, we overcome all despair, loneliness, worry, and fear. These are swallowed up because there is no fear, worry, despair, or negative emotions in heavenly places. We must rise above these to have this ascended life. When we go to the Father in this ascended life, we go alone, as individuals. We, as individuals, must establish and develop a relationship with the Father.

When we set our hearts to seek His presence, we are seeking to bring glory to Him, not to ourselves. We will be consumed with seeking Jesus, the Father, God's throne, and Heaven, and we will never want to come back. We will not return to despair, sin, lusts, bad habits, forsaking one another, and breaking the laws of God. The desire of our heart will be our relationship with the Lord Jesus Christ, and we will allow nothing to interfere with that pursuit.

### Stephen Sees Heaven

*When they heard these things, they were cut to the heart, and they gnashed on him with their teeth. But he, being full of the Holy Ghost, looked up stedfastly into heaven, and saw the glory of God, and Jesus standing on the right hand of God* (Acts 7:54-55).

Once Stephen saw Heaven, he never felt another stone, another cut, another bruise. He never felt another pain as a result of being stoned because his eyes were fixed on Heaven, God, and the ascended life. Stephen gazed on Jesus standing in glory. There was no pain for him. At that moment, Stephen was connected more to Heaven than he was to earth. He shone with the glory of Heaven and became oblivious to the things of earth.

We are called to be alive to Christ and dead to the world, just as Stephen demonstrated. Our whole being will be alive. We will be a joy to Him, and He will be a joy to us. Christ expects us to be blessed and filled with spiritual blessings in heavenly places. He desires us to have all we need.

*Blessed be the God and Father of our Lord Jesus Christ, who hath blessed us with all spiritual blessings in heavenly places in Christ* (Ephesians 1:3).

### John

*After this I looked, and, behold, a door was opened in heaven: and the first voice which I heard was as it were of a trumpet talking with me; which said, Come up hither, and I will shew thee things which must be hereafter* (Revelation 4:1).

John experienced the ascended life and saw Heaven opened. God desires for us to be with Him now. He has a remnant of devoted disciples who are willing to enter into the heavenly realm with Him. They are willing to be with Him, have His mind for the future, and receive from Him spiritual blessings. He wants us as His children to have the revelation of His glory and to live in the light of His holy presence. He has an eternal Kingdom that He wants us to learn to enter into, now.

*And now I am no more in the world, but these are in the world, and I come to Thee. Holy Father, keep through Thine own name those whom Thou hast given Me, that they may be one, as we are* (John 17:11).

In this passage, Jesus is preparing to depart. He says that He is no more of this world, but those who have been given to Him are in the world. Jesus chose to impart His glory and His ability upon His followers so that all His disciples could experience the resurrected life. He now wants us to have the resurrected life as well.

### Paul

*I knew a man in Christ above fourteen years ago, (whether in the body, I cannot tell; or whether out of the body, I cannot tell: God knoweth;) such an one caught up to the third heaven* (2 Corinthians 12:2).

Paul was raised up; he said that he knew a man who had been raised into Heaven 14 years before but that he could not tell if that experience had been in the body or out of the body. He was not sure, and he stated that only God knew. Paul was referring to his own experience. When Paul was caught up into the third Heaven, he was caught up into paradise and heard unspeakable words (see 2 Cor. 12:4). We know that Paul experienced this heavenly ascended life, and it is available for us.

This enables us to understand why there was no prison that could hold either Peter or Paul down. Once they were in prison, they were in the heavenlies. They may have been physically sitting in the prison, but spiritually, they were in the heavenlies. They could practice His presence anywhere. They could care less whether they were in or out of prison. Both men experienced God's sending an angel and delivering them from the physical prison. We can be delivered and set on high the same way. No prison can hold us, and no circumstance or sin can keep us bound if we want to be in the heavenlies.

### Ascended in Him

Once we know God face to face, we will never want to live a "descended life" again. Knowing God in the spirit of His holiness and in the power of His life, we will never want to go back to earthly living. We will want to soar with the eagles and stay with the eagles.

We have been raised up to be with Him and raised up to be part of Him. In fact, our position is to be raised up in the spirit man to be with Him right now. No one can hinder us from living the ascended life. Yet, we must choose to enter this glorious position in Him; only then is the mystery revealed, which is *Christ in you, the hope of glory.*

> *"Thank You, Father, for what You have done, for what You will do, and for how You are carrying us into a new realm and understanding of who we are in You. We thank You, Father, for the blessings that You have given us, but we thank You especially, God, for this extra special blessing to be able to visit with You in our spirit man and be raised up with You. Father, we thank You for that, and we receive it. We want to come and be seated with You in heavenly places now. In Jesus' name, amen!"*

# These books are for folks on the chase for the Lord.

## THE GOD CHASERS (Best-selling **Destiny Image** book)
*by Tommy Tenney.*

There are those so hungry, so desperate for His Presence, that they become consumed with finding Him. Their longing for Him moves them to do what they would otherwise never do: Chase God. But what does it really mean to chase God? Can He be "caught"? Is there an end to the thirsting of man's soul for Him? Meet Tommy Tenney—God chaser. Join him in his search for God. Follow him as he ignores the maze of religious tradition and finds himself, not chasing God, but to his utter amazement, caught by the One he had chased.
ISBN 0-7684-2016-4

## GOD CHASERS DAILY MEDITATION & PERSONAL JOURNAL
*by Tommy Tenney.*
ISBN 0-7684-2040-7

## WOMEN ON THE FRONT LINES
*by Michal Ann Goll.*

History is filled with ordinary women who have changed the course of their generation. Here Michal Ann Goll, co-founder of Ministry to the Nations with her husband Jim, shares how her own life was transformed and highlights nine women whose lives will impact yours! Every generation faces the same choices and issues; learn how you, too, can heed the call to courage and impact a generation.
ISBN 0-7684-2020-2

## THE COSTLY ANOINTING
*by Lori Wilke.*

In this book, teacher and prophetic songwriter Lori Wilke boldly reveals God's requirements for being entrusted with an awesome power and authority. She speaks directly from God's heart to your heart concerning the most costly anointing. This is a word that will change your life!
ISBN 1-56043-051-6

## POWER, HOLINESS, AND EVANGELISM
*by Randy Clark.*

More and more it is becoming imperative that we reach our friends, neighbors, co-workers, and classmates for Jesus Christ. But in order to be effective in reaching the lost, we need two key components: *power* and *holiness*. This is the heart of Randy Clark and the other authors who have contributed to this book. This is not about theory or theology; it is about bringing *life* and *freedom* to the people around us!
ISBN 1-56043-345-0

## Available at your local Christian bookstore.

### Internet: http://www.reapernet.com

# These books will also help you in your search for a closer walk with the Lord!

## DIGGING THE WELLS OF REVIVAL
*by Lou Engle.*
Did you know that just beneath your feet are deep wells of revival? God is calling us today to unstop the wells and reclaim the spiritual inheritance of our nation, declares Lou Engle. As part of the pastoral staff at Harvest Rock Church and founder of its "24-Hour House of Prayer," he has experienced firsthand the importance of knowing and praying over our spiritual heritage. Let's renew covenant with God, reclaim our glorious roots, and believe for the greatest revival the world has ever known!
ISBN 0-7684-2015-6

## ENCOUNTERING THE PRESENCE
*by Colin Urquhart.*
What is it about Jesus that, when we encounter Him, we are changed? When we encounter the Presence, we encounter the Truth, because Jesus is the Truth. Here Colin Urquhart, best-selling author and pastor in Sussex, England, explains how the Truth changes facts. Do you desire to become more like Jesus? The Truth will set you free!
ISBN 0-7684-2018-0

## THE COSTLY ANOINTING
*by Lori Wilke.*
In this book, teacher and prophetic songwriter Lori Wilke boldly reveals God's requirements for being entrusted with an awesome power and authority. She speaks directly from God's heart to your heart concerning the most costly anointing. This is a word that will change your life!
ISBN 1-56043-051-6

## SECRETS OF THE MOST HOLY PLACE
*by Don Nori.*
Here is a prophetic parable you will read again and again. The winds of God are blowing, drawing you to His Life within the Veil of the Most Holy Place. There you begin to see as you experience a depth of relationship your heart has yearned for. This book is a living, dynamic experience with God!
ISBN 1-56043-076-1

## THE POWER OF BROKENNESS
*by Don Nori.*
Accepting Brokenness is a must for becoming a true vessel of the Lord, and is a stepping-stone to revival in our hearts, our homes, and our churches. Brokenness alone brings us to the wonderful revelation of how deep and great our Lord's mercy really is. Join this companion who leads us through the darkest of nights. Discover the *Power of Brokenness*.
ISBN 1-56043-178-4

### Available at your local Christian bookstore.

### Internet: http://www.reapernet.com

6:35